Dishonoured
Gentleman

Dishonoured Gentleman

J. B. Kendall

JANUS PUBLISHING COMPANY
London, England

First published in Great Britain 1999
by Janus Publishing Company Limited,
76 Great Titchfield Street,
London W1P 7AF

www.januspublishing.co.uk

A CIP catalogue record for this book
is available from the British Library.

ISBN 1 85756 480 4

Phototypeset in 12 on 15 Goudy Old Style
by Keyboard Services, Luton, Beds

Cover design Creative Line

Printed and bound in Great Britain by
The Athenaeum Press, Gateshead, Tyne & Wear

I still walk the imaginary line of life
trying to grasp better things to come.
I'll walk all the roads that come my way,
some good some bad
But never in contentment, never satisfied.
If you fail like I do then get up
swallow the shameful thought and
Picture life as a battlefield:
And if ever we should not drive home the charge
or even stop to weep
Over our dead that have fallen at our feet
We would be lost
or captured by some unworthy adversary.

J B Kendall

To my Lord

For being capable of lifting such a great weight upon his back
... and then to carry it, for many miles and for many years.

In loving memory of Mum, Dad, John, who went on before.
Whose words remained little upon this earth, but their love
remains for ever ... memories.

To H.M. Forces, the army and to the Légion étrangère
(French Foreign Legion) whose Special Forces Training enabled
me to carry on when times were rough, and who accepted the
weaker part of me, but willingly shared with me some of their
technique of survival.

And especially towards you, for reading it as it was written
and for accepting it for the merit of why it was written. Thanks.

J B Kendall

Contents

Special Acknowledgements to Special People

This book is dedicated to all those special people out in this tormented world who shared with me desperate times as well as comforting times.

To family and friends who saw a greater worth in me at the end of the day, encouraging me on to write and then to rewrite the book.

To my beautiful wife Anja, without whom much of this story would have no worth. To each of my children: Rob, Annika, Mitchell (Cherre, Daniel) by my first marriage, who shared with me such desperate times in reflection on my past. To Chris (Chilly), my mate, who has always been around somewhere within my life.

But it is to Joan Atkinson (Coles), an old friend of my mother, to whom I wish to express many thanks, who saw in me only the good. To all her dear family who accepted me on many occasions to their household and befriended me on many a day; who always provided a safe house when needed and gave me spiritual comfort when asked.

To Lt-Col. Jack Mathews, Parachute Regiment, who himself has an interesting story to tell, and for his friendship and personal review. To Peter Hodgeson, a lovable person, who shared with me his love of God that has had such an impact upon my life. Truly a trusted friend. To John and Mariane Le Favre-Huisman, who have always held our arms. And, finally, to Al and Ank Napier, who encouraged me to write.

Note

This story is not for everyone and is probably best suited to those who are weak and feel they fail daily. It is a record of a journey, of a crusade within my mind towards rectifying some wrongs. I hope it is a story of courage through the tangled jungle of a confused mind. My story is of one man and yet it is for all.

I admit to myself that while writing it I was many times weakened by earthly desires and thoughts. On occasion I felt unworthy to continue but have struggled over the years to complete this book.

J B Kendall

Part One

Subjection

1

Bittersweet Memories

I am the youngest member of what was then a family of six and it is from those tender years of family life that the often bitter memories begin.

The family consisted of three sisters and three brothers: Anne is the eldest family member and probably the one I knew least about; Carol was the sister who never really was. She had married an American Air Force GI and had returned with him to the US when I was quite small, although some dim memories do exist of her being around me in my early childhood. But, like my other sister Anne, I knew very little of her and those memories that may be locked away somewhere have been clouded over.

David came next – my big lovable brother. Always at war with someone. He had a ready aggression towards the family, including my father, and yet his love for his mother was second to none. He would protect her from anything harmful. It must have been extremely hard for him to watch members of his family suffer and die around him, unable to wrestle with death itself ... but knowing him as I do, he would have wrestled for every member of his family.

John: the one I remember the most in my early childhood memories. The hunter, and like myself the great adventurer of the family. My shadow and probably the most loved by all the family.

Susan: the most level headed of the family and the one who possessed the most compassion. The one who also knows that there is something else to life than staying still and being content. The one whom I should say 'sorry' to the most – and also 'thanks' – for offering me refuge within her life while she too was in search of better things for herself. I was too young and stubborn to grasp what was happening around me and often became her millstone. On many occasions.

Mother: the most prominent figure of our family. The most honest to her children. The most treasured by all. The one who fed us and planted the spiritual seed deep within all of us – each, I guess, accordingly.

And Father – Dad: the man none of us knew; not really. The lonely figure who was despised by most of us; and yet each of us has inherited something of what he was, which we yet hated within ourselves. The man with earthly desires suppressed often by sheer depressiveness of guilt, of feeling oppressed, whose eyes were always to fill with tears of silent torture – probably not wanting to be the man he was but trying to come to terms with accepting it nevertheless.

A painful and destructive road to walk – only loneliness lies along it.

But how many of us walk this road – this road of change which we all tread – and dread.

Dad – the man that could never be forgiven by his children.

Oh, how so much am I like you, you, 'Dearest Father' and if

4

perhaps one day we could find a way of forgiveness – then please let it be your forgiveness and not mine.

The days seemed to last longer in those days. The smell of freshly cut wheat that surrounded our little village in Northamptonshire, carried on the wind, filled the air with a kind of happiness, to be shared by everybody.

We knew of no polluted ponds or forbidden areas – it was, after all, paradise. And it was ours to roam freely within.

There was no pain, no suffering or tormented thoughts of tomorrow and of its will. There was, it seemed, 'no end the morn'. The endless sunshine and warm breezes that swept this earth – death was not among us nor did it belong.

We spent most of our days scrounging through the bush, John, my brother, and myself together with our companion Champ, the little Scottish terrier who would never leave my brother's side.

I was no more then six years old. John had recently left school to begin his apprenticeship as a baker, but whatever time he had spare, we would spend it in the fields and the woods together – John, the lovable brother; the friend to us all. He was loved by my mother more than anyone.

His newly acquired shotgun did not go down well with her. It being somewhat antiquated gave her the notion to hide it from him on many occasions when he wanted to go hunting but he would be searching the whole house until he found it. It was as if the gun was calling to him in a mysterious way, desiring to be found and used...

One such day he left me at home with my older sister while he went out hunting with a group of friends ... from then on life changed.

I remember the tears and heartache, my mother crying hysterically. John had been taken away from us.

I did not know death and of whom he was.
I knew not of where he lived
Or even where he walked.
John had gone with him.

My last memories of my living brother are of sitting on a log in the field where we wandered. The rest seemed to have disappeared over the years whether through age, or whether the bitter sorrow of his death dried them up.

But surely I was too young to grasp the pain?

Time passed and I grew older. I guess I tended to cling on to my father more after the passing of my brother; often he would take me with him in his truck, travelling around England.

There were days when my mother would be doing her daily chores around the house and would suddenly erupt into tears. Pain would overwhelm her. The loss of her son would never heal; she would spend the rest of her pitiful days alone, tormented by her loss.

It was as if she was a magnificent ship, unsinkable – and yet here she was adrift, with no captain at her helm, abandoned, swept to and fro. Poor mother.

My father was not a lazy man. For most of his working life he would have no less then two jobs at the time, even three just to make ends meet for his family, sometimes getting only four or five hours' sleep. Of course we would all try and help out but we never seemed to be better off financially.

There were always arguments about not enough money to go around to buy food and the like. And there was bitterness towards my father and his ways.

I can't remember ever seeing my father's and mother's affection toward one another; and, though I never saw any unpleasantness, I felt that love was not as it should be between them.

The hurt never left my mother at the loss of John. Years went by and she would still openly weep. I don't really know if my father ever wept. He was a quiet man and had deep feelings which we as a family did not understand. He was often criticised too harshly for not showing any emotions. Towards the end of his life I felt a greater bond towards my father and I felt I knew him better then anyone else, simply because I knew what he must have gone through in his life, and that people were not always around to listen to him.

Members of my family were getting married and moving away from home. It was getting rather lonely at home now and I would withdraw to my bedroom out of sheer boredom. I was desperately longing to grow up and find some sort of adventure in life.

New term and new school. I was kitted out in new clothes to start my first day at junior level. I was chuffed. My previous clothes had more often then not been hand-me-downs to say the least; shoes were usually repaired by putting pieces of cardboard inside cut out from cereal boxes and placed over the hole in the soles – these lasted only a day or two at the most; depending on the weather.

My mother's skill at patching trousers always allowed for excuses being made for not buying new clothes for us, but this day was different. For the first time I was dressed in wonderful new clothes – I even had long trousers to wear. I felt so good, even if it was only a school uniform, it did not matter to me. I was on top of the world.

With school came new friends, lots of them; but one was to become closer than my brother or any other member of my family.

Chris was roughly my age, lived in the same street as myself and was in the same class at school, but what really linked us was that we each shared a great sense of adventure. We would have great fun together, always – though we were mischievous buggers. We would do anything other then get bored – preferably something strictly forbidden. Generally, we would rush home from school and be out and about playing in the fields or scrumping for apples in the local orchards a couple of miles away.

We weren't all bad, though; we would often go down to the brook and clear its depths of junk. And bring back little fish and such, to our parents' dismayed looks.

I guess Chris was really the substitute for my brother John. I desperately welcomed our new friendship.

Then came the big event.

A new member of my family arrived in October of that year – Tina. My mother had given birth to a baby girl. I hadn't realised that she was pregnant and now I had a baby sister. Instantly I became besotted with her; she was absolutely lovely. From that moment there began to grow a deep bond between us that was to play a greater part later in life.

Tina was born with Down's syndrome and had a hole in her heart. Instinctively I became protective towards her. The danger of her dying at a young age was always present.

John. Maybe his death had been hanging unseen in the back of my mind and only now came out of his hiding place to throw shadows over life. Tina? Surely God could not be so cruel?

God? I had attended churches and read something of him; but what was he – or who? At some stage (maybe I was ten or so) I got a Bible from somewhere and began to read bits of it, not really understanding what I read but feeling that, by doing so, I would be protecting Tina in some way. And so it was that I first prayed, constantly asking that my little sister would live and not be taken from me. Tears came easily to my eyes and often I would cry myself to sleep.

Life was still very much a struggle for the family. Trying to make ends meet was difficult enough, even more so when my mother had tremendous pride within herself and would not ask for help from anyone. She would rather suffer in silence, and only when things became unbearable would she resort to harsh words.

I would often watch her cleaning the house, scrubbing the bare floors on her hands and knees – we were after all too poor to be able to afford the luxury of carpets – and what covering we did acquire to cushion the floor was made up of old pieces of lino placed strategically around the home where our feet would tread.

The lino had rather more then one function within the household. We found out that if we placed a shilling on a really old piece of lino, and then cut around it in the shape of the coin we would be left with a counterfeit lino 'shilling' to use in the gas or electricity meter when money was in short supply.

The electricity and gas men did not seem to mind too much. They simply made a deduction when every few months they emptied the meter – they would even be decent enough to leave the counterfeit coins behind to use again. The only time they seemed to mind them being used was when they would sometimes get stuck in the slot, and they would have to come out and dislodge them.

Life was changing fast around me. I would awake early in the mornings to the sound of cuckoos calling in the distant orchards, my mind transported away to the distant lands that were part of my world and yet I had never seen. I was recognising a deep call in me, a wild call. I just wanted to feel free to be anything, aspire to anything – and achieve it.

Life was about new things to be found and explored. Who needed school? I surely didn't. From then on I became increasingly despondent, almost rebellious in my approach to any schooling that lay before me. I wanted to find out about life for myself, not be dictated to by some brainwashed civil servant.

On certain occasions when the fancy took a few of us would take the day off school. We had various haunts where no one would find us.

One in particular was the bakery – a wooden building set on brick pillars raising the whole structure from the ground, resembling a cricket pavilion but on a much grander scale. We would hide underneath the building and imagine freshly made cream cakes and bread: mmmmmm. The thought still lingers.

We would spend most of the day there waiting for the bakers to finish work around two o'clock, and then get in by the loading dock at the side of the building. There was no real evil in this. We just wanted to see inside things, wander among the machines and store rooms, curious to see how people worked.

When facing the teacher the next day, we would give various excuses; suspicion soon emerged because they would ask for letters from our parents verifying our stories. I can remember writing a letter to the headmaster myself on one occasion; of course, it did not fool him. I received three slaps on my knuckles from a stick; it hurt, and I was afraid to take any more time off whilst in junior school.

I would consistently worry over my sister; I wouldn't even stay for school dinners but would run the four miles home from school each day, just to check on my sister. It became – I became – unbearable at times. I would have violent verbal confrontations with my mother and instruct her on how to look after Tina – it was as though she was all mine, and sharing her with anyone was utterly impossible.

No one was to say a word about my obsession. She became my life; and I would take her out with me everywhere; very rarely did I venture out without her by me side.

At 13 years of age, more doors were opened to me; I was at an age where I could join boys clubs, but I opted for style and joined the Air Training Corps.

It was the best thing I ever did – it was also my first taste of military discipline. If I had stuck with it when my life took a turn on to a dark road, then maybe it would have provided something secure I could have taken refuge in. If only – the saddest words in the language. Still, for now I lived for it; and I became obsessed with the dream of one day becoming a pilot in the RAF. We would meet on a Wednesday evening for two hours and be taught about aeroplanes, flying, air force life; and weekends were wonderful. We would always be doing something, map reading, shooting, parades, attending air displays, and at least once a month flying in military aircraft. It was fantastic. Who could possibly ask for more? This was the adventure I needed in my life and I was pleased that I had found it; at long last I felt content and the future was beginning to open up all around me with endless prospects. I read numerous books on the exploits of the RAF and I prided myself in having a more superior knowledge of aerodynamics than most kids my age.

Both my parents were proud of me; especially when I was in uniform; my father took great interest in what I was doing. He had been in the RAF during the war, and would tell me

11

endless stories. I listened avidly, longing to be able to leave school and begin life within the air force.

I was about 14 years old when I was aware that things were not what they should be. My mother was often crying and I first thought that it was because of John (she never got over her grief at his loss) but it soon became apparent that a physical pain was the cause. Her visits to the doctor were increasing until one day I arrived home from school to be greeted by my older sister, who only a few months before had married and moved away from home.

She took my younger sister and myself to her home but hardly a word passed between us the entire journey. We stayed with my older sister for a few days and then went home.

Mother was in bed. We greeted her quietly and then left the room allowing her to rest. I was glad to be back home, thinking that soon things would be back to normal.

I quickly took over the household duties, cooking, washing and, of course, looking after Tina. I was actually allowed to take a week off school, it gave mother time to recover from whatever she had wrong with her.

Her recovery seemed to take ages, with many more stays in hospital, each time longer, so that in the end she was rarely at home. I couldn't understand what was going on. Tina was now at school, so she did not need looking after during the day. In the evenings it was just she and I in the house; my father never seemed to be around, it was as if we had been abandoned by our parents; I felt, from time to time, very lonely and perhaps a little frightened.

We were taken on odd occasions to visit my mother in hospital; she looked dreadful. Months seemed to go by, the strain was getting to me and I found it difficult to run the family affairs. My biggest worry was food. We never ever seemed to have food in the house. Whenever I caught sight of my father I would ask for money for groceries; often he would refuse only to return with a small can of soup to feed us. I began to feel a lot of hatred towards him and would often curse him openly. His meanness was incomprehensible.

I would hold my baby sister in my arms at night, and pray to God that my mother would recover and return home; falling asleep with tears in my eyes was very common. School became impossible. I could not concentrate on anything; I certainly could not be interested in how many wives King Henry VIII had. When things became more desperate still, I would steal money from my father's wallet at night when he was asleep, just to buy food; later I progressed to breaking into our electric and gas meters and stealing the coins.

Things being the way they were I did not get to see my mother very often. One day, when my older brother had come down from Birmingham to visit her in hospital, a neighbour looked after Tina so that I could go with him. I walked into my mother's room, but what was to welcome me was not my mother. My dear God, what on earth was going on? She awoke with slow movements to her arms as if to beckon my older brother to come closer towards her so she could hug him; they embraced. I waited to be hugged, to be told I was loved and that soon things would be as before.

'Who's your friend?' Her shallow eyes caught mine searching deep within, expecting her to recollect my name. 'It's me, Mum,' was my reply. There was silence; she didn't remember me. I walked away with overwhelming tears falling down my face. I could not stay with her, no one had told me of the seriousness of her illness. I was not prepared for this.

I waited in the car park of the hospital grounds for my brother to arrive. We hugged and tried to understand what was happening all around us, not saying anything but each of us preparing in our own way for the prospect of our mother's death.

It came a few days later. My brother simply opened my bedroom door and peered through, tears flowing from his eyes. I had never seen him cry before. 'Mum has gone' were his only words to me.

He left to be alone with his grief and I with mine. I reached for my little sister, still asleep next to me. I was overcome with hurt and loss and cried to God for comfort. It did not come.

My life was destroyed, nothing seemed important any more. Certainly my future was not in my foremost thoughts at that time; the only thing I lived for was my little sister. I had to become more than a brother towards her; she would require so much more than other kids; constant supervision and affection do not always go hand in hand.

What with all the pressures of trying to run a household and at the same time trying to cope with my own puberty and the loss of my mother, I had been denied the opportunity to grieve as I should. Instead I grew bitter, bitter that she had left us in this mess, bitter that she had not told me she was dying, bitter that my life had come to an abrupt end, bitter, above all, towards my father. This morbid hatred and hopelessness was perhaps my way of dealing with what had happened; maybe it was the only way that I could fight death on equal terms.

I would pray to God with sincerity for some kind of deliverance. This was sheer torment. Confusion! I was a walking time bomb. Still it would not come and still I prayed, oh God how I prayed.

Crime became an outlet for my frustration. I would wait until my father went to bed in the evening, put my little sister to bed, and go out into the night. Usually with my trusted mate Chris, we would reconnoitre the housing estates that had in the past few years grown up around the centre of the village. We would look for opportunities to arise – no one at home? Wham! We would force our way into any home looking for cash or anything of use to us; usually it was the electric or gas meters we went for, we would empty the contents into our pockets then quickly rummage through the rest of the house. Satisfied with our haul we would split the money and be on our way.

This became more and more frequent; what started off as basic survival for food, like the taking of bread and milk from doorsteps early in the morning, soon developed into some really heavy duty crimes being committed. It was getting out of control. But our exploits were not going unnoticed. At 14 years old we bragged a lot and somehow the police were on our tail with their inquiries. I had a bad fright and tended to stay at home during the evenings from then on, greatly worried that some day the police would catch us doing a job.

Christmas and my birthday passed without my mother being around for the first time. Tina and myself spent a few days with my sister Susan; it was a joyless affair, that first Christmas without Ma. Tears were shed over dinner as memories haunted us; from now on Christmas could never be the same, not without Ma. But there was worse to come, the more so because of its inevitability and my helplessness.

Towards the end of January I returned home from school to find the house filled with family; and to my surprise my sister Carol and her husband Duke were there. They had flown in from America where they had lived since they got married.

Duke had been stationed in the UK while serving in the USAAF, and had struck up a relationship with my sister. I had been quite young and my memories of my elder sister were very vague, to say the least. I can remember that Duke had once brought an American Air Force uniform for me to wear when I was very young. I remember all the badges that were fastened on to the uniform in true American stud fashion, the studs sticking into my body. Not a pleasant memory but a memory none the less.

I would always hear from my mother if she had received a letter from them. She would be delighted at hearing from them and made sure everybody was acquainted with their news. I think it gave her great pride that her daughter had married an American serviceman and was now living in that great Promised Land, her pride eventually rubbing off on to me. I would patiently wait in long queues outside the post office in the early mornings waiting for the doors to open. I would then walk to the counter and boldly ask to post an air-mail letter to America. The look on other people's faces gave me tremendous joy; it was as if you had to be someone very special to ask for a letter to go to America.

After the reunion of the family, the conversation turned to my situation at home. They all wanted me to go and live in America – and Tina was to go to a foster home. I was overcome with despair; I begged, I pleaded, I raged but this had all been conspired and decided behind my back. I could not believe it, I failed to see (and still do) the reason for doing this. I had been betrayed and a part of me felt destroyed. I told them all to go away and leave us alone: no one was going to split us up, I would not allow that to happen. I was only 15 years old; what could I do for myself, let alone my sister? Perhaps run away, but where to?

I packed my sister's clothes the night before she was taken away. That night was spent in endless tears, bargains to God were made, if only, if only, He kept us together; don't let this happen to us God, not this way. I would have willingly made a pact with the devil that night; I would have given my soul readily to whomsoever kept us together.

We fell asleep together for the last time in each other's arms. My fingers exploring her face, trying to reach a part of her inner soul, that somehow would she forgive me in deserting her the next morn – because, of course, she would not understand if I tried to explain; all she would know was that I had let her be taken away.

Susan had decided to be with me when the Social Service people came later in the day to collect Tina. I cannot explain how it feels when you give your baby sister away to someone else. It was as if all the deaths had come together and attacked at the same time. I tried not to succumb to tears but the more I tried the more the tears came. My insides felt as though they had been torn from me and my body felt as though my own soul had departed and I was left an empty shell.

2

The Living Death

Arranging my visa for America was done in record time; in three days everything was arranged between the British and American embassies.

It was my first time in London and, with the time so taken up being passed from one bureaucrat to another, I had little time to brood on my despair at the turn my life had taken. Self-importance at being the centre of so much attention played its part. We stayed with some religious freaks (so I thought at the time) in north London, members of a Pentecostal denomination and very Christian. My overall impression was that they were somewhat of an eccentric bunch but very warm hearted.

The house where we were staying was full of people and my sleeping quarters for the evening were in the kitchen. I shared my cramped conditions with mice or rats running around the floor and I didn't sleep well. I didn't particularly mind at the time. After all in just a few days I would be on that plane, an exciting prospect that gave my spirits something of a lift.

The first weeks in the States were a time of renewal; trying to put all the hurt that I had been feeling for many years at the back of my thoughts was not going to be easy. My brother-in-law tried to keep me busy with various tasks about the house, with painting and light building repairs; this was good for me. It was my first introduction to real work and I enjoyed it. He would tell me what he wanted doing and then leave me to get on with it, at mine own pace.

For the first few weeks life went by untroubled; my thoughts were occupied with seeing new things in this wonderful land, it was immense, and the food! For the first time in my life I didn't have to worry about where my next meal would be, or what. I would eat anything and everything. It felt good not to be hungry.

I found the Americans in general really friendly and easy to get along with. Making friends was not hard going at all; being a Limey had its benefits. My accent was what charmed them most; they were overcome almost with reverence towards me when I spoke, especially the girls. I soon became an active young lad within the church and would go two or three times a week; although I was never pressured to go, felt in some ways obliged to do so, being around a Christian family.

It was my first experience of being amongst Christian people. I was not sure of how to act towards them; after all, I came from a totally different way of life back in England.

There was so many new experiences to savour in Christian living; not all were understandable at the time and only on reflection much later in life did I fully recognise the significance of the word 'God' and what it had meant to me personally.

You know – many people claim of how God has worked in their lives and most of us are left with the impression that their lives are now superior to anyone else's. We tend to think 'That's it, end of story'. Nothing is further from the truth; if anyone was to ask me to sum up my conception of God, or to say what God means, I would find it impossible to define. I could never express in words what God was. My only hope, was that people would understand that describing him, or describing what he meant, is like describing a tree. From a distance, a tree looks graceful, of beauty and colour, swaying so lightly, free yet firmly attached to the earth.

Walking up closer things are much different. This tree is a living being, a giant in comparison with other plants; what looked wonderful at a distance has become, how shall I put it? Almost terrifying. Its trunk is covered with rough bark, like the most savage, cratered landscape, beaten by the wind and storms that have ripped deep within it, penetrating its very soul.

To the touch of human hand bares pain
Withdrawing from its form
Now I, too, gaze at the twisted shoot
Deformed from life to pierce the sky.
And tear the clouds.
Reaching, holding firm the might of wind and storm
This winding tower, its frame wrenched from a fragile
    flower,
Grave and panic.

Towards the end of the summer (Texas style) we were off to Galveston Island, where Duke and my sister had built their first church. We lived in a rather nice house built of wood, which overlooked the small church conveniently situated on a small building lot opposite.

Weekends were spent working on the church with the whole of the congregation. Taking part, these days were rewarding in many ways. It was hard physical work but we were around lovely people and close friends and the long hot days somehow had no ill effects on our spirits. Days usually ended with a barbecue somewhere on the island. Time passed by very quickly.

It was not only a time of renewal, but was also a time of deep thinking about the future. In the first few months in the US I was a real Holy Joe to say the least. I felt I was sincere at the time; at least as sincere as a 15-year-old can be about life ahead and yet, on reflection, perhaps I was a little immature in my beliefs about what God would do for me now that I was a 'walking Christian'. Sure everything would be hunkydory now. I knew that I could save the world; yep, me. I knew everything; at least everything about nothing.

It was not long, though, before I was getting frustrated again. This God thing was not all that I thought. These miracles I could perform? I could never get them to work. The unlimited doors that I could unlock never opened. Above all, the happy, never-to-make-another-wrong-move-in-your-life thing. I was always making wrong moves. It seemed that the longer I was with these kind of people the more self-conscious I became. Constantly, I was aware of the unrighteous life that I had led in England. Albeit I was young but none the less I had been doing a lot of bad stuff.

It was during the evening service – I don't know, perhaps it was one of Duke's emotional services – I was breaking up inside. I could not control my inner emotion; tears, streams of them. The only way I could avoid other people seeing me

21

reduced to tears was if I hid away in a corner. I was feeling rather embarrassed; my true nature being somewhat introverted made it even worse. What was happening? I was reduced to some screaming uncontrollable dork. It was as if there was another flood on earth and there I was only yesterday thinking I could not get the hang of making wondrous miracles to happen. Why? I'm even beginning to talk in a tongue, in fact I was becoming a master of it. 'Yo, look at me!' I was a little screwed up.

Of course I had no control over what I was doing or saying. But I was aware that something was happening to me. I felt a lot better after that, for a while anyway. Was this an experience like that at Pentecost when God's spirit was received by his congregation, and speaking in tongues was a sign of the Holy Spirit?

Whatever you choose to believe this experience changed my life. As you will see, this was not always to be associated with leading a good life – rather the contrary. Whatever purpose God had in mind, I had no earthly idea where it would lead me.

I enrolled at a Biblical college when I was still 15. I was the youngest student there; the college being some 50 miles or so from Galveston Island made it necessary for me to live on the campus. During the early hours of the day I would work in the Chow Hall cookhouse, 5.30 a.m. until 9.00. From then on until noon I would spend in the classroom, then I would return to the cookhouse and work until 2 p.m., after which I would return to my studies until five; again back to the cookhouse until 7 p.m. Then until 9.00 I would be cleaning the classrooms. I would return to my room completely shattered; after my shower I felt like doing nothing except going to bed; revision was out of the question.

About nine months or so passed living like this. My grades were not what they should have been and I was finding it harder as time went by to keep up with the other students. My depressions came back, I was beginning to question the whole damn thing. I could not talk openly to anyone about how I felt at the time, definitely not to my sister or Duke – I felt they would be disappointed with me had I had a difficulty in keeping up with the studies.

I simply wrote to my father and other members of my family that I was homesick and that I wanted to return to England as soon as possible. Eventually I had to confront my sister and brother-in-law with my intentions. I felt awkward about telling them of my decision but was firm that it was for the best.

So a couple of months passed by and I said my farewells to all my friends at the church. Again on the plane my eyes focused on the dark night, my mind beginning to wonder what lay ahead of me. The first thing I wanted to do was to see Tina. I had no idea of where she was or how she was doing, other than what my other sister wrote in her letters to me while I was in America.

We touched down at London Heathrow airport on a cold misty November day and I was met by my father, who had driven down from our home. I remember seeing his face; how old and haggard he had become.

3

Full of Easter Promise

I had arrived home with the preconceived idea of how everyone would find God. I went on my jolly way telling everyone that I was now a Christian. My life had changed – now their lives had to change. I was full of it – crap, bull call it what you want; in retrospect though, it was nothing more then complete ignorance. I had no idea of life or how it should be led. No one was interested in changing their lives; but not because of me, or what I had to say about God.

I soon became disillusioned by the Word. People were not interested in it at all. For the first time I was aware of the difference in people, from people who did believe in a creator and those who didn't, and of course the ones that insisted on proof. I had nothing to offer. Where was this God? The one that had promised sanctuary? The miracle maker?

I lasted only a short while in being open about my beliefs. I had learned to avoid ridicule by my friends by keeping my mouth shut. In so doing it wasn't long before I was back to my old self. No work, no money. I had got back with my old mates again; we would regularly commit some sort of crime. We would spend our gains on drugs and booze; it got worse by the day. My father would tell me not to associate with the like of my friends, but I would never listen.

I tried getting a job but that only lasted for a few days. I was becoming hopeless: I had no control over my life; drunken brawls, stealing cars, breaking and entering property, violence to others, nothing seemed to matter. It was easy to get a reputation as being hard and fearless and, in some ways, it brought with it a kind of respect from others, or at least I thought of it as such. It was probably during one of my less frequent days of being sober that I thought of leaving my home town. I was getting frustrated with everything and I could not hold down a job to save my life. F*** it.

I left home on a cold winter's day, destination Lowestoft, Suffolk. Why, don't ask me. I just had to get away from my home town to see new faces. I only had a few pounds on me when I reached Lowestoft, enough for a room for the night. It was pouring with a chilling rain and I was very weary, cold and hungry. In the morning I would look for something to do.

A nice breakfast greeted me at the table, tucked tightly into a corner of the lounge of the B and B. It had been a long time since anyone had cooked a meal for me and I was going to enjoy every bit of it. I looked around Lowestoft and found myself down by the harbour; all I could see was what seemed to be hundreds upon hundreds of big fishing trawlers; it looked wonderful.

This was it! I called into one of the many trawler owners' offices that lined the wharf off Waverley Road in Lowestoft and got myself a job as a deckhand trainee. It was that easy. My employer booked me into the Seaman's Mission that stood adjacent to the docks, where I was fed and kept until I had undergone shore training and learned the basics of becoming a deep-sea fisherman.

The shore training lasted for ten days. I quickly made new friends with the other guys who had the same inclination as me to be a deep-sea fisherman. We were introduced to our instructor, Skipper Soames. I can still envisage him quite clearly in my mind's eye, a short stockily built man, partially bald. He was somewhat aged but possessed such a radiant look about him, his face weather-beaten over the many years that he himself had spent at sea. The salts of many oceans had ripped deep within his soul, and had carved for themselves a unique figure of a man. A fisherman. Rough. Tough. Fearless. And yet he possessed a warmth and gentleness worthy of a saint. When he spoke in his soft voice, you would know that you would be secure in this man's knowledge of the sea.

We all passed a basic test. At the end of the training period everyone was looking forward to going to sea; we were taken to the shipping office and allocated a ship. Luckily most of the trawlers were out at sea and were not due back until later on during the following week.

We were given a few days off. Time to put in an appearance back home, I thought, and with the money that I had earned from the training period, I caught the bus home for the weekend. I visited most of my family but stayed away from my friends. I knew that if I was to hang around with them that I would somehow get into trouble.

Deep down I knew that there was a better life on offer and I wanted to keep it that way. After all, it had been a big step on my part, to up and go, and I was determined to make a new life for myself.

It felt odd to go and see my little sister in her new adopted home. She had memories of me still. I had felt that a visit from me would be an intrusion on her new life within another family – the pain would have been just too much to bear. Especially when I felt I could offer her little comfort.

At least a couple of years had passed by since the last time I had seen her, and I was confused about how I would react at seeing her again. It was awful to see her with another family. It seemed that every time we looked at each other, our eyes would meet head-on. She would pierce the hidden depths of my soul with her gaze, searching for the answer of why she had been taken away from us. I felt an agonising guilt at what seemed to me an accusation, as if I had been responsible for the events. I had no answers for her, no words of comfort, for I too was still looking for these but had not stumbled upon them. My visit was brief. I could not sit there, my heart aching. Oh, how I wanted to hold her close in my arms again, to bring her home.

I can no longer bring myself to see her, not because I no longer love her or think of her. It is solely for the reason that I could not face her.

I left a day earlier then expected, back to Lowestoft. I reported early the following day to the shipping agents. I was crewed up on a boat that was to put to sea in two days' time. I was told to report to company ship stores (or chandlers). There I was kitted out with all my clothing for the two-week voyage at sea. We were allowed to order contraband within reason: books, chocolate and cigarettes, etc. These were placed into a kit bag and a small wooden box, and carefully marked with our name and the boat we had been allocated to sail on. It would be placed on the quayside, alongside the boat the same morning of departure, ready for us to collect. It was, I guess, some kind of company ritual, that they would be seen to

27

care for their crew. The same way, a mother or wife would care for her loved ones before they journeyed off to work or to war.

I had a restless sleep the night before I set sail, worried that the boat would capsize or something like that would happen. It was still dark when we left the Seaman's Mission to walk the few yards or so to the harbour gates. Floodlit ships were silhouetted against the dark morning sky but it was already busy on the dockside, with members of other crews trying to find their ships. It was a windy day at that, with a storm brewing up.

I was beginning to doubt my intentions of becoming a fisherman. With each minute that passed looking for my ship, my stomach was pulled tight with the nervousness of departing for the first time on board a ship. What made it worse was that I had a bad case of flatulence. With each step I took I would fart; 'S***, that's all I need.'

And there she stood, elegance afloat, the *Roy Stevens*, my first ship and, as promised by the chandler, my gear alongside her. I grabbed my belongings and almost ran aboard the ship. Already most of the crew were either on deck, or below, stowing their gear away.

I found the first mate and reported that I was aboard ship and ready to roll. Roll! That is an understatement. The weather was absolutely awful, and that was on a good day.

The colour of the sea changed as we steamed into deeper waters, as did that of my vomit. Ah, I was seasick. For three whole days I could not venture out from my bunk, only making frequent journeys to and from the toilet which was inconveniently situated at the stern of the boat, making life very unpleasant in rough seas for everyone who did not have their sea legs.

It was the engineer I shared a cabin with who convinced me

to go and have a good greasy breakfast. Not that it made me feel any better, only that it was better to be sick on something rather than nothing. From then on I made a point of having a large breakfast before setting sail. It does help.

Two bells at intervals signified work. Trawl time. I ventured on to deck, ready to do the stuff. I was greeted by huge 50-foot waves; it was unbelievable, the immense size of the sea and us being only 125 feet in length made it more difficult to comprehend the sheer expanse and volume of water that threatened to engulf our very lives.

If ever beauty looked into soul of man then this must have been it. The sea has such possessiveness; in her entirety a living being, unwilling to part with her secrets, only on rare occasions to permit some to see her hidden treasures.

I felt that the huge sea had eyes and that they were somehow looking into mine, searching for confirmation that I was indeed worthy to be on her fleshy waters. And to fish at her soul and therein to take part of her spirit. A spiritual experience and I'm afraid that, unless you yourselves have been to sea in a rather small vessel and had the privilege of looking up to the huge waves of our seas and oceans, you will have no comprehension of what I'm trying to put on to paper.

We would search for the fishing banks, and lay our nets over the side. Trawling for hours at a time catching tons upon tons of fish. My job was the same as the rest of the crew – to muck in and help each other out. Casting the nets, repairs to the nets, gutting, filleting, keeping watch, cooking, working in the ice room, etc. It was very hard work but I soon got the hang of things and began to settle in quite well with the rest of the crew.

While the *Roy Stevens* was undergoing a refit I decided to sign up on another fishing vessel, the *Suffolk Craftsman*. She was a side trawler, which meant that her nets are put out to the side of the ship when fishing. This vessel was in a class of its own, clean, more room and even had washing facilities for the crew, including a shower.

The crew was special from the first moment I boarded her. I felt accepted and I stayed with them for the rest of my days as a deep-sea fisherman.

Life aboard ship seemed to suit me. Lots of different things to learn and always somebody to talk to. We were a bunch of jokers to say the least, right up to the captain, which made life a lot easier to cope with while away on long voyages at sea. There was always someone playing practical jokes, none of us was immune or escaped any form of tomfoolery or abuse by another member of the crew. On occasions salt would be put into the captain's tea in place of sugar, or a rotten fish would be placed on a hot part of the ship's engines, sending a very unpleasant smell throughout the whole ship. Boots were stuck to the floor, even fish was put into someone's bunk. Just foolishness I guess, but it was fun. You never told anyone if you had played a joke on somebody else, that was the secret, though trying to keep a straight face for the remainder of the voyage sometimes became an impossibility. There was always somebody who became overwhelmed with laughter at one stage or another before the ship had docked. The captain, however, would always put a stop to things before they got out of hand. He knew just how far things could go without anyone going overboard.

Our catches were often low at the beginning of the voyage, and really depended on where we fished. I can remember many times when we had in fact no fish in our nets; also others when we had unexpected catches. Once we hauled aboard large amounts of German and Danish beer, obviously some cargo ship had lost it overboard in rough weather. We learnt that you need to be careful bringing up such a catch; bottles are prone to explode after lying some way down in the depths of the sea for long periods of time. You never knew what might come up in the nets: bicycles, prams and the faithful shopping trolley guaranteed to be found anywhere. It was a real treasure hunt at times, making it more interesting.

We would usually be out at sea for about two or three weeks at a time but this depended largely on our catches. Most vessels operate on a share basis, giving the crew a percentage of the total amounts of fish caught and sold at the fish market; most fishermen opted for this system of payment in Lowestoft, as you could earn extremely large amounts of cash and we all wanted to be rich, especially when we were back in port.

Our social agenda: most of the crew would stay together and go on a drinking binge lasting days rather then hours; we would literally throw money away at various venues. Others would wine and dine the ladies of the night, who always lined the harbour walls. They would be on the quayside as the boats came in, waiting for the crew to disembark; there would be a rush forward and a lot of tugging took place, each eager to satisfy this or that lonesome seaman. As you can imagine, wild parties often ended up in violent scenes. The police cells were full of fishermen, who had been drunk and disorderly, or who had just simply lost their way in a fog of alcohol.

I was no exception, of course; and it was on just one of these binges ashore that my life took another disastrous turn.

One morning I was awakened by a British Rail police officer in the early hours of the morning. Somehow I had ended up on a train with another crew member, and under influence of drink, we had robbed the bar of all alcoholic drink and had completely demolished the interior of the

31

catering car, then foolishly fallen asleep in one of the first-class compartments on the train.

We were sober enough to give false names and addresses to the police officer, but didn't hang around to be handcuffed. A slight shove of the shoulder I'm afraid, and we were off the train.

We hid in the fields until nightfall, then we split up and tried to make our way back to the ship. A few moments later I watched my mate being picked up by a police patrol. These guys meant business. I took a homeward route; if the police were going to pick me up, better on home ground than here.

4

Chin Up! Quick March!

Being back home was not really what I wanted after a week or so I decided to try and enlist in the RAF. No such luck; they would not entertain me. I had not completed school and possessed no academic qualifications. They told me to reapply when I had gained a little more education – fussy buggers!

I was getting impatient again and was missing the life of a fisherman, but too scared to go back to Lowestoft and face problems with the police. No. I'm afraid I couldn't hang around too long back home. There was only one thing to do. I went to join the army.

The Grenadier Guards. I was not really given a choice of regiment to join – the recruiting sergeant made up my mind for me. All I wanted to do was get away, so I didn't quibble. Within two weeks I was on the train, destination Pirbright camp in Surrey.

I was unaware of the history of this famous division but was soon awakened to the fact. Every morning we were reminded that we had not really enlisted into the army, but that we had in actual fact joined the *Guards*, the elite independent brigade. This meant nothing to most of us other than it could function independently from the rest of the British Army if required to do so. That was what we were told endlessly by our instructors.

We had the most soldiers in any division. Five regiments of guardsmen infantry, two regiments of cavalry troopers, one being mounted troopers, the others being armoured. This was what was commonly known as the Household Division; within the division they had what was and still is known as the G Squadrons – the Independent Parachute Regiment, the Pathfinders and the Special Air Service Regiment.

Standards were high for the guardsman; even the bullshit had to shine. Great emphasis was put on physical fitness as well as neatness and being efficient in everything we did. Training was difficult; if you didn't shape up to the high standard required you were sent to a less respected regiment. It was not long before we were all brainwashed into thinking we were the lads. I suppose it gave us instant recognition and pride; two of the most important ingredients to develop loyalty among fighting men of any armed service in the world.

Although living conditions were somewhat spartan, they was not uncomfortable. As to the food, I had never been so spoilt for choice; it was extremely good. The first few weeks of training were the worse. Everything seemed to be in chaos, including ourselves. Our kit was never in our lockers or put into cupboards, no, it had to be neatly arranged on our beds for all to see. The only time it could be put away was when we were allowed to go to sleep.

Endless inspections, from a variety of staff; from the lowest of ranks to the top nobs of the army quadrants, everything had to shine. And, if it didn't, everyone would suffer the consequences, enforced by members of the instruction unit.

Nothing went perfectly, there was always something wrong; even if it was a hundred per cent right they would dress you down and make a complete fool of you. You would think that they would let up after a while but it got worse; they expected more out of you. The only thing to do was to function like a robot, forget being an individual. The regiment didn't want individuals: it wanted a machine.

You kept your mouth shut and never ever dared to question (thank God the British Army has now developed more responsible behaviour towards the fine men who volunteer to serve). This was still the 1970s and your worth was judged only on your capacity to triumph over the physical and mental stress; the recruit would often find that brute force was often the only thing that mattered.

The weeks flew by during recruit training and, before we knew it, we were ready to pass out and go and join our respective battalions somewhere in the world. I felt proud to have completed the training but very sad that no one from my family had bothered to come to the passing-out parade. I was the only guy who had no one to talk to after the affair; from then on I felt pretty well isolated from the rest of my family and friends. I just kept myself to myself; they were not interested in my life in the army and, to be honest, I wasn't really bothered about theirs.

I thought of the time when my mother had died; none of them had attempted to console me in my grief, not one of them had bothered about keeping us together as a family. It made things worse for me, because I really loved my family, but felt nothing in return. Call it self-pity, call it what you want, I was only 17 years old and still in need of love from someone.

From the time my mother passed away, I've felt nothing but being pushed away from my family. They would only condemn me for getting into trouble; in the life I was leading they had no idea of how I had to survive sometimes; unaware of my being unable to eat for days on end; oblivious to the hurt I was feeling inside of myself. They had no concept of how it feels when someone departs before you can tell them you really loved them. No idea of how it feels to watch a loved one taken from your very arms into another family; no idea of how it feels to see all of these things and be too young and frustrated to do anything about it.

Life with the battalion was almost as bad as rooky training. Because I was new, very often all I had to do was the crap, like extra guard duty, or fatigues. Unless the battalion was on exercise, life was tedious.

I hated being in camp, and found it difficult to settle into the regime of things. Most of the guys drank too much and gambling sessions went on until the early hours of the morning. This was definitely not for me. I had regular visits with the OC (Officer Commanding) to see if there was something else I could do within the battalion – my requests were shelved along with so many of the other lads' requests.

It got so bad that on one occasion I told him I would like to see someone higher up. I got bollocked by the RSM and thrown out of the room. But within a week they had pulled their fingers out of their arses; somewhere along the battalion echelon and I had been selected for training with the G Squadron.

I was given ten days' leave before the course started, so another home visit was on the agenda. I don't really know why I decided to go home at that time; after all none of them ever wrote, although my father would occasionally put pen to paper and write a brief letter to me. It was obvious that I would stay with him while on leave; I took things easy for a while before I saw anything of the rest of the family or my friends.

Everyone had changed from the way I had remembered them, from what now seemed ages ago. Each had his or her own life, and I was soon aware that my life was no longer important to anyone other then myself.

Although my father and I were not the best of friends in those days, he too had his life to lead. We did sometimes share military gossip with one another; he had spent most of the war years with the Air Force and enjoyed telling me about the times he had. Poor Dad, I had forgotten about him – he must have suffered through all of this, and this man had few friends; definitely no family. They had long ago forgotten him and had deserted him. They were all quick to give their reasons, but I could never understand why they had so much contempt for him.

Selection and training for any independent airborne force within the armed forces throughout the world produces elite professionals. The British Army is by no means an exception to this. I had in fact volunteered to become part of this small nucleus within the army and any punishment I received within my body or mind would be well worth it; after all it was only training.

I quickly learned that I wasn't super-human in any way at all. Often I would make mistakes and take too many chances but at the end of the day I was encouraged by my tutors to realise my mistakes, make good use of them and carry on. It was tough to endure when my body was weak – it was tough to survive when I just wanted to die.

A few weeks passed and there was a significant drop in the participants of the course – from 40 volunteers there were only 20 of us left, and this was only the third week of the course. Most of the reduction was due to medical problems, with men not being extra careful with infections obtained during training, such as burns to the hands and inner legs which, if neglected in the field for long periods of time, become septic. Up until week three most of the casualties were due to light wounds or infections that could have been prevented. I guess at the end of the day we were already trained soldiers before we volunteered for G Squadron and it was expected of everybody to keep his body in good working order and to seek medical advice if he had any real problems. Some of us didn't and paid the price – RTU (Return to Unit), the candidate returned to the regiment whence he came.

From then on we were given scrupulous medical checks by the MO for blisters and the like that could prevent us from carrying on with our course. After week three, which consisted mostly of getting rid of the cobwebs from our previous postings by means of physical exercise, we began to learn more about survival and campcraft and how to live in the wild, eating such exotic things as mice, rabbits, worms etc. Eating them was the easy part – knowing where to find them and then catching them, that was the skill.

On one occasion we were dropped off on our own; this is where you are dropped off from the back of the truck on your own in the middle of nowhere, in the wilds and in complete darkness. You are unaware of where you are, as your journey in the truck was also in complete darkness. You have at your disposal your map, your clothing, and a grid reference you must reach within three days; it's up to you to reach your destination. The rest are dropped of at intervals of around two or three miles to reduce the chances of meeting each other along the way.

The Brecon Beacons in Wales was to become our second home from home during most of our training and offered our instructors unlimited recourse to test our motivation. Doing something on your own was only one of many exercises thought up by the instructors. So here I am cold and wet and feeling somewhat bewildered at being left completely alone, and I mean alone.

We had been given no prior warning of this event and no time to reflect on past and forgotten map-reading experience. It was assumed that, already being trained soldiers, we were competent enough to use our heads. I was hoping that I would hear the next candidate being dropped off by the sound of the truck slowing down further up the winding dirt track. I crouched beside a tree and some rough bracken gave me some comfort in protecting me from rain and wind while I listened to the dying sound of the truck.

This was the first time I had been alone for quite a long time, and I became afraid of the situation. Usually we had been together with at least four to eight soldiers at a time, but this was different. Within minutes of me being dropped off by the others, I began to panic, desperately trying to remember what I should do, everything and nothing were beginning to race through my head. Shit, I had to take control of the situation. I was left with only the sounds of nature, and with the ghostly shadows of the trees that were being tossed by the storm in all directions.

Assessing the situation: it was dark and very wet. I had no

means of illumination, torch or matches, and no idea where I was. I stumbled around for a while trying to find my bearings or to search the hillsides for lights, a house or perhaps a distant town or village within easy reach. It was more of a comfort thing really and a state of mind; if I saw a light, then I would feel reassured that there were others around me and that would give me a sense of security, however small.

I began to remember the basic survival techniques we had learned a few days before. Moving away from my initial drop-off sector and into thicker cover within the bracken bushes, I decided to lay low until daylight. I gathered branches along the way which had been torn off the trees in the storm, and burrowing into thicker bracken made a 'basher', a kind of beehive shelter with the branches and leaves to give me some protection against the wind and rain.

I felt for the map and the coordinates which I had put in my left pocket – nothing, absolutely nothing – shit! I searched for what seemed hours, and then ventured out of the security of my basher, searching the path I thought I had taken; again nothing.

I crawled into the basher and began cursing everything about the army and my life. I got to the stage of cursing myself when I realised that I had in fact placed my map inside my combat jacket knowing that it would have become soaking wet had I left it in the outside pocket. Again profanities were upon my breath. I was totally out of it. Confusion, utter confusion; what a complete tosser I was.

I drifted off to sleep shortly afterwards, only to be awoken at intervals from droplets of rain falling from the leaves above my hide. I guess they had become saturated by the storm and the sheer volume of water that had collected on them, and forced the branches to sag.

I was beginning to think that I had made another mistake in volunteering for this sort of crap, but it wasn't long before the sky lightened and the sun was rising. Time to get on with things.

I washed as well as I could with what water was left on top of the leaves to remove the awful stench of mixed sweat and damp clothing. By the time I had finished the sun was up. Ideally I should be moving in the dark and lying up by day, but it didn't really matter as I wanted to have a good look around, to see exactly what was about me before moving out. Often in the dark the surrounding area becomes distorted by the shadows and it becomes easy to get disoriented and, with no navigational aids at my disposal other then a soggy map, I was not about to take unnecessary risks.

I quickly disposed of my basher, making sure that no possible traces were left behind of me ever being there; then, moving to higher ground, I began to evaluate the surroundings. I tried to look for prominent features on my map that would correspond to the landscape, hoping that I would get a rough idea of where I was and where I was heading.

It took a while before I found where I was and in what direction I had to travel. I marked the spot on my map where I had to be for the pick-up point with a light touch of a twig but a bit off the actual area, so as not to arouse any suspicion in case I got caught by anyone who was out there looking for me. Should that be the case and it usually was, then I could be ready to deal with it. I had long since learnt: 'Always expect the unexpected.' And since evasion techniques had been taught to us in basic training I implemented them with great care.

I knew that if I was going to be ambushed I would definitely be asked where I was going and where I had come from and, if they got hold of my map, they would know where our

41

rendezvous was going to be and ambush the whole platoon – so I wasn't going to help them.

Over an hour must have gone by before I felt confident enough to move on, keeping to the high ground as much as possible so at least my observation of the surrounding area was not restricted too much, and at least I could make a run for it if I was spotted.

The distance was not too great to cover in three days; some twenty-five miles. I decided that from time to time I would backtrack just to satisfy myself that I was not being followed.

Two days passed without much difficulty or unexpected encounters. On the second evening, I was disturbed by noises. I had made a bivvy of sorts quite early in the evening while it was still quite light. I thought that I would spend a few hours in the light rummaging around trying to find food and water, but I had made an OP away from my bivvy and it was from there that I heard voices. There was more then one person talking and I lay low among the foliage hoping they would pass. But they decided to spend some time near where I had put up my bivvy and it was quite late before they moved on and later still before I dared venture out. I did not go back to my bivvy that night as I was not sure who they were; they might have been other lads on the same course who had met up at some point along the way, but I was unsure and did not want to break my cover.

I spent most of the night foraging, careful not to make unnecessary noise. I thought that I must have walked about two or three miles, occasionally seeing moving lights of some sort; had I walked into a concentration of the 'enemy'? Cover was getting a little sparse now and I thought of playing it safe and retreating back some 300 or 400 metres. I decided to remain there for the night, bedded down as best I could and gradually dug myself into the long grass.

Morning brought with it a sense of urgency. I had to assess the situation carefully; I had twice the previous night brought possible attention to myself and had been lucky that no visual contact had been made. I arose carefully from the long grass, making sure I did not break the sky line. I watched cautiously for any movement and listened for noises; it seemed quiet enough to move forward just to the edge of the end of the long grass which has given me some protection during the night. There I had a better view.

Again reaching the edge, I lay outstretched with my arms out in front of me and carefully parted the growth of long grass that was hiding me. The way ahead was clear, but what worried me was who was behind me and what lay to the left and to the right. The only way I could evaluate the situation properly was to try to reach higher ground and survey the area. But where was the high ground? I had walked some distance during the night but really had no inkling where higher ground lay.

I retreated back into the undergrowth and paused awhile. What to do? Should I stop imagining there were others out there trying to prevent me from reaching my rendezvous? Perhaps I am getting paranoid? No sooner had the thought entered my mind than all hell broke loose. In front of me thunder flashes (imitation grenades) were going off with long bursts of machine-gun fire. I froze, not daring to move.

I was stunned. The concentration of noise was relentless. I knew that if I suddenly moved and ran for it I would be picked out and hunted down. 'S***!' Everything was rushing around in my head. I decided to wait a while and listen to what was happening.

43

Na – they would have ambushed me surely, avoiding all the commotion and noise? This seemed like an exercise from a secure OP where the opposition would throw some kind of bombardment or light fire into an area of cover and hope they would drive infiltrators into confusion or panic so as to create movement, a tactic used commonly throughout the military. Once movement can be observed, a good spotter can direct his commands of fire to prevent withdrawal; he can, if desired, eliminate them with ease. But on this occasion he seemed to be only sweeping the area at random so I knew I had not been spotted. I stayed put.

Ten or so minutes seemed to go by. The noise had panicked someone – I heard voices, so I crawled cautiously to the edge of the long grass and peered through. There they were, three captives, I could distinctively make out one of them from my platoon. They were no more than 50 feet away and being manhandled by six men. The firing continued but with odd intervals of silence. I could hear questions being asked – how many other guys were trying to reach a rendezvous and where it was. I could not hear their answers, and then they were being dragged off towards some sort of vehicle that was coming towards us on the open track adjacent to the field; obviously the section had requested some form of transportation back to their HQ where the prisoners would no doubt be further interrogated.

I made a slow crawl to where they had stopped some hundred metres away. They were being tied up and blindfolded, and placed on the ground awaiting the arrival of the vehicle which had just pulled alongside them, but directly in front of myself. I withdrew slightly into the long grass and backtracked a few metres to where I thought I would be in a less exposed position to observe the situation.

A stroke of luck – most of the patrol had gone about regrouping with some other formation towards the top of the field and were quickly out of my sight. There was only one armed guard and the driver left to deliver their captives back to their HQ. I had a perfect view and began to think about a rescue attempt. I could quite easily pick these guys off in a real combat situation but reality was something else. I had nothing other than a little dare-and-do to offer any of the captives, and as for a plan of action I had to wait hopefully for an opportunity. The prisoners were loaded into the rear of the vehicle and placed belly down in a head-to-toe fashion.

Again negative thoughts. I really had no purpose in even contemplating any rescue attempt. It was not my fault they had exposed themselves. I should really leave well alone and concentrate on my own situation. After all, if we were all caught then it was more probable that we would all be rejected and RTU without any further delay. They had only themselves to blame for getting themselves caught. Leave well alone.

The firing had all but dwindled away and a sense of normality had returned. Birds now ventured to return to their haunts and were going about their business. Again my eyes focused on the situation. One of the guards was laughing while the other reached for his cigarettes in the breast pocket of his combat jacket, only to be distracted by the squelch of the two-way radio in the cab of the vehicle. Obviously someone wanted to know what was happening to the merchandise; the conversation was brief and scarcely audible; I was unable to make any sense out of the conversation that had taken place. Again I decided to play the waiting game, for an opportunity to present itself.

45

Placing the radio back in the cab he then instructed his accomplice to get into the rear of the vehicle and keep an eye on the catch. I began to think that I had just better lie low until they had departed.

Again he reached for what I thought was his cigarettes in his top breast pocket. I couldn't believe it – he'd only fished out a bog-roll. What the f***? He strolled casually over towards where I was lying on the ground, passing within only a few feet of me, and slowly turned around. He had his back towards me and walked one or two paces further, where he stopped. Removing his army webbing and putting it to one side, he began to undo his trousers and lowered them to the floor. His ass was parked almost over my legs as he began to manoeuvre and crouch for his shit. Not over me, mate, and with that thought I reached towards the back of his combat jacket and pulled him back so that he was lying completely on top of me. With the other hand placed over his mouth, I quickly rolled over him so that he was on the bottom and I was on top of him.

I was glad no one was around. It would have looked as if I was trying to give him one up the arse. It was imperative that I took charge of the situation; aggressive behaviour does have its benefits on occasions and this was one of those moments. The driver was in total shock which was good. He was momentarily paralysed and I proceeded to tie his hands and feet together with part of the webbing he had placed beside him. He was beginning to react by now and becoming aware that he had been ambushed. I quickly gave him a knock to the head to remind him to be quiet. I also gave him words of comfort before I tore his sleeve from his jacket and gagged him with it. I took his hat and put it on my head and tried to look something like a driver who had just taken a shit. I slung the remnants of his webbing around my waist and over my shoulder, making sure it was left undone and, picking up the toilet roll, I walked toward the Land Rover keeping an angle of approach slightly off from the vision of the guard so he would not get a good look at my uniform or manner of dress. I walked around to the jeep, removed the webbing and swung it around so that it would hit the guard in his face and stun him. In his confusion, I removed him from the vehicle and disarmed him. After telling him to get back in the jeep I told him to release the prisoners. I then took control of all the men, dispatching two of my team to collect the driver hidden in the field.

The two guards had now become our prisoners and we took them with us in the back of the Land Rover. We were all a little bewildered, and really had no time to discuss our plans of action. I drove the vehicle across country as fast as possible, throwing the R/T into the rear of the wagon and ordering one of the guys to find out some 'intel' about the intention of the opposing side, and where they would most likely be positioned along the route.

We had some advantage in that we could listen to most of the radio transmissions being broadcast and to some extent we did try to confuse them with our own transmission on the net, using the driver's helpful voluntary services. We drove on as far as we possibly could; our main objective was to put as many 'clicks' (kilometres) between them and us. Beyond that we weren't thinking about anything too much. We abandoned the jeep in some woods and camouflaged it well by deliberately driving it through some thick bushes, thus immobilising it. We decided to take our captives with us.

We walked only a few clicks before we decided that it was too risky to travel in daylight, so we hid inconspicuously in the shelter of some wooded area until it grew dark, when we would force-march the few remaining kilometres to our pick-up point.

It was a typical army f***-up – they were late, or we had misjudged our rendezvous; whatever, they were not where they should have been. We did not hang around too long, withdrawing into the bush and setting up two observation posts, or OPs, to the north and south of our position; this would give us some protection in case we were ambushed, the plan being that only one man would expose himself to the identifying body who was supposed to be picking us up, and then inform the others that it was an OK contact.

This was a vital course of action and in the end proved its worth. We were constantly in danger of being spotted by our rivals, endless patrol cars were near or about the vicinity. It was tempting to stand up and walk towards them, thinking that they were on our side and that they were looking for us – no, no, no, of course they were not friendly, someone must have spilt the beans. They were all around us like swarming bees; we watched in silence as others of our unit quite openly mistook them for being friendly and gave themselves up.

Out of 20 guys, only six of us didn't get caught in this confusion. Back at our improvised barracks for a debrief, the OC was not a happy man. He was not impressed with the overall event especially when most of us got captured. He threatened all of us with instant RTU if we didn't improve our standard.

We all knew that some extreme form of physical endurance task was to be dished out in retribution. We stood at attention for over an hour waiting in the freezing cold. By now the morning light was coming through: 'left turn!' and 'double march!' TAB fashion across the mountainous terrain for five or six kilometres; reaching a fast-flowing river we were told to swim across.

It was ice cold and all of us felt weak and threatened by the event. I think had it not been for the fact that sometimes you could touch the bottom with your feet, some of us would have been swept away down stream seriously injured or even worse. I began to question the motive behind this foolish order, knowing that most of us had not eaten for some days, had been exposed to the elements and were suffering from fatigue. I thought it foolish that an officer would even contemplate sending men into ice-cold water just to prove his authority.

Reaching the other side finally and with great difficulty, we again assembled into an orderly fashion before setting off on another TAB back to the barracks. At last a hot shower, clean gear and a good breakfast – all in five minutes. I wondered why we actually volunteer for this stuff. I could find no logical explanation. Why is it that men feel so motivated while suffering physical and mental torture and abuse just to be part of a pathfinder unit?

The course began to intensify – long marches across the moors and, with each day, what we would be expected to carry in the field would increase. Our 'burgens' (large backpacks) would sometimes stretch under the weight of what we would have to carry, slung on webbing, which consisted of a waist belt and various straps that would be attached to the yoke (harness) that would envelop our whole upper body, with the additional pouches fitted around the whole contraption. Usually it was worn loose but then bits would fall off when on the move or, even worse, the whole thing would disassemble itself on the march and end up wrapped around your feet. When wet it became uncomfortable and cumbersome.

49

A great degree of time was spent on navigation during the selection period and this was often carried out at night, with great distances having to be covered within an allotted time. One of the most gruelling events was on one of many evaluating stages towards the end of the basic selection test. This is where the candidate has to cover 45 miles within 20 hours carrying at least 83 pounds' weight; if you failed this you were either out or were dropped back to be re-assessed later. Which of these largely depended on whether you were liked by the training staff.

The final week of assessment, and now down to only nine of us left. Things were a little easier now on the physical side of things; what had seemed like an endless competitive athletic event halted. We were given endless reviews and personal interviews at various levels of command from the lowest up to the highest and we had to satisfy all. Another week of waiting around and then we were called up to the OC. He briefly told us that we had been successful and congratulated us on our success on gaining entry but stressed that this was just the beginning. Proper training would begin in ten days' time at another venue. With that we were told to enjoy what days we had free and to report back in seven days' time, this time in our maroon cherry beret. We were in.

Although the basic selection process was over, life within the regiment didn't stand still for one minute. There followed intensive courses in weapon training, tactics, unusual combat scenarios, where we would put into effect resistance-to-interrogation and evasion skills, and then a few months spent in the jungle before being whisked back to the UK.

We were still very much rookies and ages seemed to pass before I felt accepted by the other guys within the squadron. This is usual practice; others tend to give you the cold shoulder for a while, until they feel confident of you and accept you as one of the family.

No. 1 Parachute School, Royal Air Force, Abingdon. Although this stage of training was important and well disciplined, its methods were new to most of us. No longer did we have anyone shouting at us if we did something wrong or suffered being punished like little kids if we failed in anything; instead we had masters as instructors rather than aggressive animals. We were treated like human beings.

What a difference, to be instructed by professionals who never lost control and who never ever dreamed of screaming at an individual who put his foot wrong. The RAF and its methodical teaching has had a great deal to teach the other services and will always hold a special place deep in my heart. Their motto 'Knowledge dispels fear' lives up to its name.

The parachute course lasted four weeks and covered a multitude of things. Whatever could go wrong during a descent was explained thoroughly by the parachute 'jump master'. He put a lot of guys' minds at rest with his soft-spoken instructions during the first week of pre-drop training, safety precautions, how to land and fall, fitting the chute and finally the balloon drop.

Your first real jump is from a balloon; everything prior to this has been simulated. The balloon is raised to a height of around 800 feet and suddenly you're there looking down, suspended in mid-air in a creaking cage, swaying from side to side and with it your insides, everyone being thrown about and by now most of us were having second thoughts about jumping.

'You.' 'Me?' 'Step forward.' The dispatcher instructs me to put my arms across the reserve chute. I really don't want to jump now. 'Go!' and I am gone before I can think. Training has made it easy to jump on reflex to an order; before I realise it, the chute has indeed opened, as promised by the PJI, automatically. It takes approximately three seconds before the main static parachute opens fully and for me to check the canopy has deployed correctly. Another three seconds should be sufficient to deploy the reserve chute should a malfunction arise. I am supposed to count away the seconds on my downward journey to earth – 'one thousand, two thousand, three thousand, check canopy.' No way. The sheer exhilaration of dropping into emptiness confuses the brain momentarily and I am left trying to catch my breath. By now things are happening pretty fast. The ground is coming quite close towards me and then suddenly I remember what in fact I am meant to be doing while up there, the ritual. Check canopy and steer away from the balloon cable by using the lift webs. All-round observation and everything appears well. The adrenalin is pumping, your heart's throbbing and you're dripping with sweat. Feet together, elbows and shoulders tucked in and what's this? Ah, my balls have dropped back into place from my mouth. Someone is shouting at me from below giving orders and instructions over some sort of PA system as to where I should be landing, but with all these strange sensations I'm feeling for the first time, my mind is far from the instructors on the ground.

Within a short time I'm back on terra firma, struggling with the lines to collapse the chute quickly before the wind takes hold and drags me all over the place; eventually placing it into its bag and throwing it over a shoulder while walking over to the PJI for his comments.

Jumping from an aircraft is different. The whole sensation changes and you certainly feel more secure and in control. Every jump was different, height increased and our equipment was more and more elaborate. Towards the end you realised that being parachuted about the place was only a form of transportation; what really mattered was what you did on the ground when you hit it. Everyone loves to drop in on a situation and it looks spectacular but, in all seriousness, the novelty soon disappears especially when the parachuted soldier's life expectancy is only calculated at three minutes on the battlefield.

Life with the squadron was interesting to say the least, unlike a conventional unit where a lot of soldiers' time is spent in boredom. I find that too much routine in the army has a negative effect on the morale of troops. They become complacent and non-effective in a situation. I was happy that I had managed to get out of a conventional unit.

The squadron was organised into special sections, depending on its many functions. However, everyone was expected to be able to do another man's job and be capable of a multitude of skills. It takes a minimum of two years to retrain a trained soldier to be capable of operating on his own initiative in a special forces unit and to get the best out of him. These units, like their men, are exceptional but it's strange that they still have to depend on scrounging around other units for essential equipment to maintain their operational readiness; G squadron not excluded, and even it, on occasion, had to rely on its own funds to purchase new and better equipment.

My service years took me around the world to some of the least exotic parts, from the Middle East to the streets of Northern Ireland during the 1970s when the Troubles were at their peak. It was probably on these streets that I became more aware of what was happening to people and to myself. I was questioning everything I was doing, aware of the deceptions of the politicians.

I didn't agree with all we were instructed to do and became

so disenchanted with things that I just wasn't functioning properly; this became apparent not only to myself but also to my OC. I was changed deep inside of me. My thoughts became troublesome – I didn't want the kind of man that I had become, but I didn't know what I wanted to be. I was desperate to change, but into what? I had no idea; confusion gripped me from within, wrestling with my thoughts constantly. It seemed so long ago that I had a complete family at my side, but not so long ago that I could not still feel the pain of bereavement.

I would study other people around me – had they had such a hard life as me? Had they also been plucked up by a wrath of God, twisted and thrown down so early in their youth? Did they have anyone to love? To hold? Were their thoughts of tomorrow or of yesterday and of how cruel life is? Could any of them compare their lives with mine? I seemed to be the only one who had such a troubled life. I began to resent everything about myself.

Others that I was associating with while engaged on special duties seemed sometimes bizarre but they had the knack of accepting what they were or had become. They would carry out any function they were ordered to do and sleep peacefully that same night with no regrets or remorse.

I wondered why I was beginning to change, questioning the real motives behind our ops in Northern Ireland and the violence we administered often so casually. Why was it that only I was doubting? Surely there were others who had experienced this? I had no idea of the history of the Troubles in Northern Ireland and, to be quite honest, I didn't even want to know. I was sent to do a job and I did it the best I could. I took orders just like everyone else, and carried them out as most of us did, but why the confusion in my brain? Was this stress? Sure you get to see some horrific sights; mates go out and fail to return; others are trying to kill you as you are trying to do your job; kids throw Molotovs, screaming women spit in your face and throw verbal abuse at you, and this was from both sides of the community. You were in the middle of it. Right up to your neck.

Obviously some of the guys had been involved in this longer than I had. They had grown accustomed to the never-ending petty violence that had gripped the entire nation. Forget the religious beliefs of the Catholics and Protestants, it had a much more sinister side to it than that. And unfortunately everyone suffers. It had become volatile and political for all parties and the army seemed to be at the receiving end of all the anger.

We were all guilty of making mistakes at the end of the day, each of us as an individual and each of us as a nation. Why on earth haven't we learnt to forgive? We seemed to be classified in endless pigeonholes and labelled; is it any wonder that we act accordingly? The army is no exception and consists of men and women who at the end of the day are only men and women.

In the same mysterious way that I gained entry into the regiment, I left. My recollection of the unit is full of pride and of great respect. A big thank you in helping me overcome life's difficulties and pressures whether for the right reasons and even for many wrong ones. The knowledge and the many memories told and untold will remain with me.

5

Living the Lie

Leaving the army was probably the biggest mistake I could ever have made but my conscience led me to seek another path; as to what, I had no real plans. My mind was in turmoil, anxiety quickly set in and I made a decision to go home and rest for a while before making any permanent plans for the future.

It didn't take long before I met my old mates again although everyone seemed to have changed. Most of them were engaged in criminal activities and the more I associated with them, the more I became involved. Everything about my life was to become distorted.

I decided to enlist in the Territorial Army. They were keen to have me around, having had experience in the regular army; but it never was quite the same. Most of the guys dreamed of going to fight somewhere and becoming instant heroes; their talk was small and they would waffle into the early hours over beer in the bar above the drill hall. Here I was, having come out of regular service disillusioned and tormented by some of the things we had to do as serving soldiers, now to be faced with endless chitchat from guys who knew nothing of real soldiering but lived in hope of one day being called upon.

All I wanted to do was have a quiet life, with perhaps military connections along the way and, having spent a few years within military realms, I thought it best that my life should continue with a little discipline being applied even if it was only at weekends. Of course this was short lived – during the week I would find myself being part of the criminal fraternity, and the two didn't mix.

Work was non-existent. Sure, I tried but no success at the end of each day made it more and more difficult for me to get out of bed in the morning. Was this really what civvy street had to offer me? Factory after factory, the majority shoe manufacturing. This was not for me. I've never considered myself as lazy, although there have been times when I've found myself relying on welfare. My problem has been never finding a dream that I could commit myself to. I've had thoughts and aspirations, but they have never ever transpired. Most dreams cost money, unfortunately, so I must learn to adapt and survive in the environment that today's society has produced.

Perhaps if nothing else I've learnt how to adapt to situations that life itself has thrown my way, most being unpleasant and even shocking, but for which I'm the richer. I firmly believe that there is a greater power at work within each of us if only we would acknowledge its existence, call it 'God' or 'fate' or even spiritual awareness, call it what you want. What matters most is that we recognise it and accept it; understanding it is impossible, so don't waste your time. I've tried over many years to comprehend the endless questions that are to be asked; there are very few answers in reply. Even scholars and professors, scientists and great religious academics can't agree; at the end of the day, we still have no peace.

My life was declining fast into the underworld. I wanted money, and from petty crime, justifying it as basic survival of the times, I turned into a ruthless crook, wheeling and dealing, into everything. Drugs, burglary, car theft, robbery with violence, it didn't seem to matter. And yet I did not feel good about doing it, any of it; but my need seemed greater than my doubts.

Making the headlines in the local newspaper was new and for a while, each week would bring with it a new story condemning my life. Great personal shame was felt deep within, and the only way I could deal with it was to do something more bizarre. I was totally out of it and lost my personal control over my life.

The authorities were not amused by my behaviour either and with a criminal record as long as your arm, I was sent to prison. Eighteen months of mental torture and living in shit. Never ever did I imagine myself ending my life in a prison. The journey from Wellingborough to Bedford prison was spent mostly in silence and with the solemn thought of being kept locked away for so long a time. It seemed as if it was for ever. I was ready to run for it should the opportunity present itself. No way was I going to be locked up by anyone. Bastards!

Resentment at the authorities was overwhelming; I had a great hate for all concerned and I didn't hide the fact from anyone. It was on a dark winter night that I entered the large gates of the prison; my first impression was that of Colditz prisoner-of-war camp during the Second World War, as portrayed on television. The narrow steps for the convicted prisoners to the reception rooms of the prison had been worn down over years of use; the walls on either side were painted in depressing browns and greys. At the very end was a barred gate leading to another locked door. The rattle of the keys that were being menacingly sorted through by the prison guards, the turning of the lock and then the door being opened – the world beyond these locked doors that have been left unseen for centuries had now been opened so I could see clearly.

The shouting of the prison staff greeted us in the same fashion that I had become used to in boot-camp in the army. We were all lined up in single file and accounted for. Gradually we were individually seen by the PO who would then tell us our sentence and verify our names and addresses etc. We were then instructed to remove all our clothing in front of the staff, who in turn would list our clothing and place them in a moth-balled boxes. These were then stored until we completed our sentence.

Being a convicted prisoner I was not allowed contraband. Any cigarettes or money etc. were to be placed in a large brown envelope to be sealed and kept somewhere safe within the prison. We were then directed to a small cubicle where we were told to put a bathrobe on to cover our naked bodies; there we waited for hours until the prison doctor and medical orderly arrived, again stripping off to be looked upon. Touching my toes and then having the cheeks of my arse parted and being closely eyed, I felt like farting in his face but refrained on this occasion.

After the brief encounter with the doctor and his mate, we were led to another part of the building for a bath. Six grand iron baths stood neatly in a row, individually divided by a small partition that offered little or no privacy to the great delight of the prison orderly who stood watch as you bathed.

A bar of white Windsor soap (prison issue) would then be flung in the tub just as you began to place your hand over your genitals to cover what exposed part the nosey ponce found fascinating to stare at. Within no more then a couple of minutes I had to vacate the bath again into a cubicle where I dried off. Another nosey asked my clothing sizes and with great efficiency I was clothed in prison costumes after which I was herded into a cell shared by six other guys to await allocation. The cell measured no more then eight foot square with a small barred window at the top of the room offering no ventilation at all. The whole process of reception took hours to complete and no food or drink was available until the following day.

What the f*** was I doing in this place around these guys? For the first time, reality began to sink into my thick skull. I had become a degenerate. I felt sorry for myself, pleading silently within myself to God that somehow he would intervene and get me out of this asylum. I was making all sorts of bargains with him and I was sincere. I would have done anything that first night in prison, if only he set me free.

Finally, we were unlocked to be taken to the big wings of the prison itself, where the other scum of society were housed. En route we were issued our bedding and plastic piss pots, shaving equipment (no razor blades) and one clean set of underwear. Everything was placed into a green or red bed-spread and, by holding the four corners, we were ready to continue our journey through the endless maze of corridors leading to the main prison cells. Already I was pissed off; still no intervention from anyone. Someone soon would realise that they made a big mistake in sending me here, I wasn't a criminal, no, I had a jolly good reason why I had committed my crimes. It wasn't me. I'm innocent, ask anyone.

60

The last gate that led us from the reception area to the main hall was slightly wider than all the rest. It offered a frightening view of the prison complex: the steep spiral steps that led to the landings that housed the row upon row of cells as far as one could see; the netting that separated each landing in its entire width and length was designed to catch those who would carelessly fall from the heights above; it had a menacing look about it and added to the already tense atmosphere that greeted me as I passed through the gate.

The echo of it being locked again seemed to linger on. It was no more than a big cage, the problem was, I was inside it. I had been allocated to B3/17; this was my cell, my home. My God, what had I really done to deserve this? I entered my cell at around 9 p.m. that evening to join two other guys who had nearly completed their sentence and had only a few months left.

Our introduction was brief; name, the crime and our sentence was all that passed our lips at this stage. Rather like the army in many ways, with name, rank and number. I felt awful that night and just wanted to hide away alone and call out for help from God. He was the only one who could help me now; this prison thing was obviously real, no one had made a mistake.

I was here all right for being a complete asshole. It took me about ten minutes to put all my prison gear away on the few remaining shelves and to bed down for the night. The lights went out around the prison at about 10 p.m. I lay on my bed staring at the shadows that were cast by the outside security lights that shone through the small window at the top of the cell. There I cried deeply within myself for being in this situation; I was pleading with God to help in some way to change my life.

I didn't want this kind of life and yet I was not prepared for any other. It was all I knew – if things didn't seem to go right then I would turn to crime for an easy result. I had no knowledge of the hurt I must have caused to others and, if I was aware, well perhaps I would have still committed the crime: I was unable to help myself. I had a tendency to turn to God expecting instant miracles of him and if they were not instant then I would step into action and really screw things up.

From early childhood I was under the impression that God was unique in this way. He could do anything. I still have this belief but now with the knowledge that time alone is on God's terms and not on ours, and he alone knows the time to answer and to reveal. But this was then and I had not learnt the many blessings that were to be bestowed upon me or of the greater understanding that the years would bring.

I awoke the next day earlier than the other two inmates that I shared the cell with. I lay in the silence, my thoughts drifting back to childhood days when all my troubles some-how didn't matter. The silence was only broken by the sounds of the pigeons that were nesting all around the prison; it was the only reminder of freedom that was left for me.

It wasn't long before the prison officers were banging on the doors and making a count of the convicts; the prison was now beginning to breathe with all different sounds that I had not heard before. Lots of shouting and vibration shook the walls as if the whole structure was a living monster that had been disturbed. Perhaps it was only me feeling anxiety, worried about what prison was really like.

'Slop out! Pisspots and jugs only!' The door was unlocked

and flung open, there was a rush for the open door by the other guys each carrying a jug and his plastic piss pot eager to be the first to empty the contents down the drain before the overwhelming stench filled your nostrils and made you physically sick.

About fifty cons were queuing up at the urinals waiting to do their stuff (one sink, one piss hole, one crapper, to see the needs of so many men, this was the 1970s. Or was it?) I had never ever been greeted with such disgusting conditions, especially in England. My immediate thoughts took me back to the Middle East and the poverty that was rife throughout the oil-rich lands that I had visited with the British Army – the smells were almost the same regardless of the baking hot sun that scorched the buildings. There too one would have to stand in line to use whatever amenities were available. I really wasn't looking forward to doing my bird (time) in this place.

The first few days were spent out and about seeing different kinds of people within the prison establishment; medical personnel, the education officer and, of course, the governor. I got put into a workshop sewing mail bags for the GPO and the railways, eight stitches to every inch. There were about 20 or so other cons doing the same sort of work for about one pound a week. Meeting different people offered some relief and took my mind off the outside world. The pound a week enabled me to buy a few small luxuries like tobacco and sugar.

There were no radios in those days. Any entertainment came only once a week, Saturday morning cinema, and chapel services were offered on a Sunday morning; other than that you stayed behind closed doors. Not being used to staying in one place I volunteered to do extra work like cleaning the shit house and the landings. It was not pleasant work but at least it got me out of my cell for a few hours a day. Not only that; I could earn yourself a little extra contraband running messages to fellow cons that were locked away in their cells and found it impossible to relay messages to one another; on a good week I could find myself possessing at least an ounce of baccy extra. Tobacco is gold within prison and I quickly learnt how to survive within its walls using cigarettes to obtain almost anything.

Prison has its own humour embedded deep within its walls and is almost indescribable unless you have been through the mill yourself. Even with the tormenting memories that haunted my thoughts there were occasions when I could laugh. After I had served my bird. For me, looking back it was probably one of the most trying times of my life both physically and psychologically. And if everyone had experienced it before they were so willy-nilly about sending people off to these places then our prisons would be less inhabited.

My discharge didn't come soon enough. I left with only the clothes on my back and about £20 in my pocket. I had not got a clue where I was going to stay that night or what I was going to do. Most of my other mates were themselves serving time somewhere and had not yet been released. I went back humbly to my home town hoping that some member of my family would take me in for a while until I got myself sorted out. No go, I didn't get a look in. They all made their excuses and I really could not be bothered with crawling up to them any more than I had done, so it was a case for the probation services to sort out. What a mess. I was placed in some sort of B and B.

My bed reeked of beer and piss and was damp from whatever. Ah shit, I didn't want this. The next morning I attempted to eat breakfast amongst the hundreds of cats that were roaming about the dining room; my table was neatly overlooking the un-emptied litter tray that even the cats seemed to ignore.

It appeared that I was the only client in the house and was made a fuss over by the grossly overweight landlady who, on closer examination, resembled a female Santa Claus, if there is such a person. She was dressed in a red tight-fitting tracksuit that had never been washed and her face was heavily made up with a texture that can only be described as Artex or plaster. Her beard – yes, even a beard – was an inch long in places I swear, but her disposition seemed to be friendly enough and persuaded me to endure these living conditions for a couple of more days at least until I could find something else more fitting.

I struck lucky as it happens, and none too soon – the landlady had taken quite a fancy to me. I was rescued by an old soldier mate who invited me to move in with him and his family and who actually got me on my feet again with work and the like. Being a taxi driver was probably the first job that I thoroughly enjoyed since leaving the army and I worked at least 18 hours a day seven days a week for a while. I began to think that life was beginning to look up for me; but within a few short months I found that I was again out of work and money was quickly disposed of when I had it, on drink and having a good time with the women.

Memories of prison were far behind me and I chose not to remember the ordeal that I had previously gone through. It became unbearable when I couldn't get work, especially in a small town; my reputation had preceded me; everyone knew that I had been in prison and they would not take me on for work. Although I had been going straight since being discharged from the nick, nobody wanted me as part as their work force. I tried everything you could imagine but always with the same answer – not suitable.

I was really getting pissed off with things by now and decided to move away again and try my luck back on the fishing boats or oil rigs. Perhaps being in a different place would change my luck for the better.

I decided to try Lowestoft first, perhaps I would see some of my old acquaintances and maybe they could put in a good word for me. Getting a job was going to be an act of faith and positive thinking on my part; I really had nothing too lose at this stage and took the gamble to search for work. I reached the main bus depot in Lowestoft with only about ten quid in my pocket. My possessions were all in on old suitcase fastened with two pieces of string so it would not fall apart.

Stepping off the bus into the rain and the memory of having done this before some years ago in similar circum-stances made me feel a little more secure in that at least I knew where to look for work. I walked down to the railway station some half mile away from the bus depot and placed my belongings into a small locker where they would be secure for a while and I would at least be free of the burden of having to carry them around with me in my search.

The first thing I thought of doing was going to the welfare to see if I could get a small amount of money so I could at least get a room and some food inside of me. What a carry on! I joined the queue of the unemployed and waited and waited and waited. It was already gone four in the afternoon before I was eventually seen by one of the staff and, having stated my situation to them, was refused any help whatsoever – until I had a permanent address. I told them that I could not get an address until I had some money to pay for the rent but they were adamant and would not entertain my request for help. It became a Catch-22 situation, resulting in me having to live rough on the streets while I tried to get work.

So I spent most of the evenings in train or bus stations in the hope that the following day might bring with it a change of fortune. I must have looked a mess when I asked for work; my diet had consisted of only a light breakfast during those few days and I longed for a good hot bath or shower. Again I decided to try my luck with the welfare people. The same situation arose when I told them that I had no permanent residence although they did give me £30 on this occasion because I informed them that I had at least got myself a job. I hadn't, but I was getting desperate for money just to buy decent food to live on and I thought the little lie was justified to get some help from the system.

The first thing I did was to collect my belongings from the lockers at the railway station and then to book myself in at a cheap B and B and have a good hot meal and a bath and then ponder on what I was going to do. It was hopeless to stay in Lowestoft any longer than was necessary; since arriving I had noticed that the fishing industry had been dramatically cut down. It was no longer a thriving community of fishermen and seafarers and the fact I had recently been discharged from prison did me no favours with the local people; so what else, back on the bus and to another location.

I thought maybe London would be better for me to try my luck, it did offer more chances of work surely, after all it was a large city. After paying for the B and B and the bus journey to London I was left with only a couple of pounds in my pocket and knew that again I would have to approach the DHSS and ask them to help in finding some sort of accommodation for me. It was the same old thing here – crowds of people of all ages asking for help, endless waiting about and getting no sympathetic help from the staff. I was really getting fed up with this s**** life (all I wanted was to get a job, anything).

The doors were locked behind me as I aimlessly walked down the steps of the welfare building with nowhere to go. The weather didn't offer any compromise in its reluctance in easing off the icy rain and I was soaked through to the skin. My suitcase was beginning to hurt my hands and arms having been held in them for such a long time in the bitter winter night. God, why was all this bad luck happening to me? For God's sake someone help me. Look at me – I felt I had been reduced to the lowest form of our society and all because I was searching for a better life.

In the doorway of a shop stood a lone policeman. Pride had disappeared from my life – I walked straight up to him and asked with tears in my eyes where I could find shelter for the night. The policeman's reply was all I needed to hear, especially in my state of mind. Try the Salvation Army hostel in the next road. He placed one hand on my shoulder and with the other he pointed, to where it was hidden out of view from the norm of society. I felt no reluctance in approaching the Sally Army for a bed. That night I felt finally beaten by what life had done to me over the past years, and all I wanted to do now was rest awhile and rethink my life and direction.

I awoke in the early hours of that night to the sounds of men groaning in their sleep, obviously troubled with something deep within their souls, their torments were audible throughout the remainder of the night and I began to inquire silently within myself as to why so many men were troubled in their dreams. I inquired further when at the opposite end of the room someone was pissing on the guy in the next bed. This was not real was it?

I made no further attempts to find explanations that night

and finally drifted off to sleep. I really was past caring about anything. The following day all my questions were answered in full. I was surrounded by tramps and junkies, mentally ill grannies and bummers – you name it I was amongst it.

Was this to be me? Had I trodden so deep a path that I too, was to end up like this? I sat on the edge of my bed analysing each of the people who had shared the same room that I had been in, my thoughts going back only a few years ago to when I was a proud member of one of Britain's most powerful elite forces. They had tried to break every part of the character I possessed as part of special forces training and had only made me stronger at the end of the day – and now this. It seemed ironic, the millions of pounds the government spends on the military training of its troops, and yet here we are or at least me, now a civilian, broken both physically and mentally in trying to survive in this urban confusion of bureaucracy – and the training hadn't cost the government a penny.

I was wondering where all this would lead to eventually; and knew that somehow I had to change my circumstances, but how? I was completely alone. I seemed to have done everything wrong in the past and nothing seemed positive in my future. I was living a day-to-day existence and somehow could not perceive enough of the future to influence what lay ahead. I endured staying at the hostel for two further nights, the maximum that anyone was allowed to stay at one time in each week; London it seemed, attracted everybody. Why on earth I ever chose to go there in the first place eludes me.

For the next month or so I lived like a tramp; the nights that I could not spend under cover would be spent walking the streets of London, carrying my trustworthy suitcase, with old newspapers tucked into my clothing offering some warmth to my body. I would try to find a suitable place to sleep but more often than not ended up sleeping in someone's garden shed or in a derelict building that was infested with rats and mice. On endless occasions I approached the many churches that abound in and around London asking for some encouraging word of what I should do. No one offered consoling words of comfort or gave me food when I asked, although one vicar did go out of his way and gave me a glass of orange squash before politely telling me to leave the grounds of his church. My faith in mankind dwindled to an all-time low and, although I was constantly angry with God during my ordeal, I would still silently pray to him and ask for his intervention in helping me.

The strange thing was that most of the comfort and food I was given came from common folk who many of us would label as ungodly and undesirable and who had never even stepped inside a church. Perhaps many people who attend Christian meetings have become too pious in their thinking and have forgotten where they themselves have come from. Whatever, I can't explain their excuses.

My path took me eventually away from London and back towards Northamptonshire, but not before my strange encounter with Arthur. We met at Victoria bus station some time in early April as I was waiting for the bus to Northampton. He was standing in front of me waiting for the same bus when he suddenly turned around and asked me to look after his small suitcase while he went to the booking office. I thought nothing of it and didn't think it too strange a request as he was getting on in years. He returned after a great deal of time had passed and by which time the coach had arrived and the passengers were already boarding. We were among the last to be seated and were happy to be on our way out of this jungle and quickly struck up a friendly conversation. Before long he knew my life history and still remained friendly towards me. He invited me down to Wales where he lived on a huge farm.

After a few weeks in Northampton I decided to visit him in Glynneath, South Wales. I was looking for Mr Arthur Jones of Pontygwawthog Farm, and having been directed by a passerby who knew of him personally I took the long road up to his farm. It was situated in the forest and was nothing that I had imagined it to be. I thought that he would be able to give me work and he did.

The farmhouse was constructed of two old railway guard vans that were joined to one another. He had no running water – this had to be collected from a well at the bottom of the huge field in the middle of the forest. All toiletries were done in the bush except during the evening when we would share a bucket.

He didn't possess any modern-day luxuries such as TV or radio, in fact he was a complete recluse, an eccentric man to say the least. He had gifts of fortune telling but more, he gave me spiritual help in again finding a path to choose in life and for a while he comforted my troubled soul.

I was to spend the rest of the summer on the farm doing what work I wanted and going for long walks with one of the many dogs he had acquired. Although the time on the farm gave me a chance to recover somewhat from the stress of living rough on the streets, I knew that I must soon be on my way to find a life of my own and to walk upon the wheel of fortune and at least try to find my destiny.

Back in Northampton I managed to find work in a shoe factory and hated every day of it. But at least it gave me some independence and a chance to recover some of my lost

71

dignity. It was also a time of meeting new friends who themselves had some inner belief in a God; it was interesting to listen to other people's accounts of how they had found security in their own sanctuary of a firm belief; for me it was different, my belief in God changed as frequently as the seasons. I realised that with each experience I went through, or had to overcome, my concept of him changed. I felt I was constantly wrestling with the whole idea of a God whom I didn't really know or understand. I felt troubled when asked my opinion of him by others who had been around religion for most of their lives – my answers were only of what I had found personally to be true and for the most part I had become disillusioned with Christian doctrine as a whole.

Most people had the thought of God and knowing him came only from historic accounts from the Bible. Mine were simply from trying to survive in this world on a daily basis and getting caught up in reality and all its evil voices. I guess that I was fearful on many occasions of losing my faith in God and with the whole concept of religion but again on reflection perhaps it was only my nerve that I lost in not truly accepting him. Perhaps that is why I seemed to be running away from life.

It was also a time of finding feelings for a woman. For the first time my inner passion exploded and I was allowed to explore a woman's body and to experience the warmth and comfort of being intimate with someone who actually told me that she loved me. We would spend the whole of the day making tender love with each other, often resulting in both of us being reduced to joyful tears of compassion that could only come from deep inside the inner soul. For the first time I felt secure and madly in love with a woman.

She was 15 years my senior, divorced with two children, but

there was no place in my heart to harbour any doubts of my feelings towards her. Doubts came later in our relationship when I had to collect her from the local police station, drunk and disorderly. It was becoming a big problem and I had no real idea how to cope with the situation, I had no one to talk to about my doubts that had by then progressed into jealous suspicions that she had found someone else. I was frantic with fear of losing her to someone else.

The long process of losing someone again took a turn for the worse this time around; twice I was admitted to hospital having attempting to take my life, once with drugs and once with a razor. This time I really fell by the wayside; the agonising hurt felt too deep to repair and once again I took to crime. This time with vengeance – I was fed up with living on the breadline and having to work long hours of the day for next to nothing in return. I had tried to live a straight life and had struggled to overcome my weakness as a man and was doing my best to hold some Christian beliefs in my life, but all of this seemed to be worthless and I felt I was not achieving anything in life through being such a goody-goody. It was as if I was destined in life to lose whatever I struggled to achieve.

For the best part of that year I became a con-man with all sorts of schemes operating. The main banks being keen to give credit, I was everywhere but not really going anywhere. It quickly got out of control and found myself living a Walter Mitty existence. My identity varied in different towns along the way along with the tall stories I was giving people; in one place I was a respectable company director and in another I was a high-ranking officer in the security realms of the military – this was the easiest identity I could play; after all, I knew something about it.

Hotels were no problem. I would book in for a week or so

and then simply disappear before they knew what had happened leaving them some bogus company to pick up the bill. I usually operated alone and was more confident in doing so; only if it was really necessary would I involve somebody else.

It was probably the involvement of others that caused things to go wrong and eventually I relied too much on their help; a lot of scams didn't come off, and we changed our tactics and left the con-market alone and concentrated on robberies or high-class burglary.

Thankfully, we were all eventually caught. We were arrested by armed police officers after they had pinpointed our hideaway (a safe house). We were ruthlessly taken away to the nick only to be told that they were looking for another gang and had mistaken us as part of them. It was too late to make any excuses or denials of what we had done; we were given prison sentences of five and three years.

I took a deep breath and tried to compose myself. How I hated to be caged again. What on earth was I doing here again? The familiar processes were the same as before, the prison rituals had not changed and again I was left with the tormenting punishment of being incarcerated alone with my thoughts – exactly what was it designed for. God, how I hated every minute of it and I still had 18 months to go. From when I first arrived I planned somehow to escape from this hell-hole; this time I was not going to stay and if people were to get in my way then I would be prepared to use whatever force I had to, to regain my freedom.

I wanted out.

I was sent to a low-risk semi-open prison somewhere in the Leicestershire countryside, Ashwell, an ex-army camp with old wooden billets that housed the prisoners in a dormitory fashion. You could roam the place with relative ease and even the prison officers were laid back. The only security was the large high fence that surrounded the prison compound but, what the hell, I had learned how to penetrate security fences.

It was shortly after our last evening roll call before we were allowed to get into our pits, that I decided that this night I would go over the wall for real. I was given five pounds by a con whom I had befriended and he wished me luck. With that the lights went out and the doors were locked for the night. I quickly disappeared towards the toilet at the other end of the room and with the help of my mate, I lifted the wooden floorboards and dropped through to the cold ground below.

It was not long before I was looking back towards the security lights that shone through the mist that shrouded the prison complex; it was quite spooky and often when I turned around I thought that there were people in pursuit. I had become disoriented and was really unaware of the direction I was heading in. I saw only reflections in the night sky of a small town that was some way ahead and decided to head in that direction, making sure I kept to the fields that offered me some protection from view. It was quiet and all I could hear from time to time was the sounds of dogs barking in the distance.

I felt it was best that I alter my pattern of escape from walking in roughly a straight line into something of a zig-zag pattern just to throw the scent a little if I disturbed anyone. It was heavy going. Each field I took was newly ploughed, making it the more difficult to traverse; putting distance between me and the prison became a more difficult task than I had thought. Somehow I had to find a less troublesome route to follow, otherwise my endurance would fail me and I would begin to make mistakes. I had walked and crawled for what seemed an eternity before I felt the softening of the ground below turn into something more desirable to the feet and quickly made away from the fading lights of the prison towards the town.

From there I would be able to telephone a taxi and with the five pounds that I had been given at least get some of the way to where I was going. I had managed to persuade the taxi driver to drop me off close to my home town of Wellingborough and walked the five miles or so to where one of my mates lived. I was sure he would assist me for a few days or at least until I got my head together and decided what to do. I had been hiding there for three days when I heard unusual noises around the house. Looking out of the window I saw a fleet of police vehicles had surrounded the house; I called for my mate but no answer came.

I quickly ran upstairs and no sooner had I reached the top than the doors were breached simultaneously by the police. I had no real time to react, the only thing I could do was the obvious – I dived under the bed.

The police were in the house some 15 minutes with dogs that passed by me licking my face as I lay in silence under the bed. It was not until they decided to give up the search that one of them had the idea to lift the bed and that they found me.

I went back to jail (high security), tormented by thoughts of where my life was leading me. I was a hopeless case whom nobody could help. My mental state deteriorated and I found it difficult to conform to prison life in general, and sudden outbursts of violence made me a regular visitor of the block (segregation facilities). Being fed on only bread and water for periods of time only made me more difficult to control.

By now I had spent more than five years of my life inside prison and the thought of freedom soon became a nightmare of where to go and of what to do. Although my past had seemed somewhat checkered in the way that I'd lived, no one would ever know the truth about the real me, of how most of the time my life seemed to be taken over by another personality. I was aware of the evil I was committing to others around me, I seemed to have no control over the actions that bore with them such devastating consequences to those around me and, of course, to myself.

The last few months of my prison sentence were spent in deep thought of how I could break this great tribulation of my criminal past and maybe somehow put straight my path in the decisions I would make in my future.

I had to break loose from the grip of the criminal fraternity. I had no idea where to start looking for help, not that I would have asked for any. This really had to be done on my own and with this sincere thought I prayed to God. I knew that miracles take a little longer to work and I didn't mind the wait, but what I thought would take weeks to perform turned into months and then into years.

My waiting for help from God has taken me on a great adventure to the far extremities of this planet. The experience I have gained through waiting and *wanting to change* has lead me on paths I knew not I trod until I was made to stop and look back to reflect and to accept.

> A seeker of silences am I,
> And what treasures have I found.
> If this is my day of harvest,
> In what fields have I sowed the seed,
> And in what unremembered seasons?
> If this indeed be the hour
> In which I lift up my lantern,

It is not my flame that shall burn therein.
Empty and dark shall I raise my lantern,
And the guardian of the night shall fill it with oil
And He shall light it also.

6

Marche ou Crève

I arrived at the Gare du Nord railway station sometime in the late spring, on my own and carrying my worldly possessions in my trusty suitcase. The only address I had was Forte Nogent, Paris, France: a recruitment station for the Légion étrangère (the Foreign Legion). It seemed to be the only choice I had left; it solved the problem of where to go and what to do and, yes, I joined to forget.

Contrary to belief, they do not take anyone within its ranks; they are quite selective in whom they enlist. I am nothing special and have never thought otherwise; I simply told them my life story and the problems I had with the law, and that I desired a better life if given another chance. The one thing the Legion will do for any man is to give him a chance, and sometimes more. Providing you are completely honest with them, then they will protect you. Whatever your past has been, whether you are a has-been or even a never-been, the Legion will find something for you to do. Provided you pass the necessary requirements:

79

Identification: the French love bureaucracy at its best and do like to know more than you would care to talk to them about. You don't give them bullshit, it's a non-requirement and the Legion doesn't deserve to be misled if its sole purpose is to help you to succeed. A new identity is commonplace within its ranks, if so desired – your choice.

Medical: providing you are healthy then you are getting closer to enlistment. It doesn't stop there; there are frequent medicals along the way and there is still a way to go yet.

Nationality: any will do except French. Absurd, isn't it? Most Frenchmen become French-Canadian in order to comply with the legal requirements for enlistment into the Foreign Legion. I told you, the French love bureaucracy. Its officers must be French; although now I understand that there are exceptional circumstances to this.

Security: a brief session with the Security and Military Police. Just a general talk on a casual one-to-one basis. Remember, no lies and no bull. Lectures about the Legion and its ops are at this stage given in private; only when the Forte has more than five candidates within its walls does the laid-back nice approach give way to a more rigid military regime. It then becomes apparent that these guys require some input from you and this is before you have signed on and are getting paid.

The days are getting longer now. Maybe it's because you are getting up around 4 or 5 a.m. or maybe it's because you are not lying around the place doing nothing. At this stage you can still walk out if you're unsure of the commitment that is required by the Legion.

About a week has passed and we've now been joined by other hopefuls from around the country at various pick-up points arranged by the Legion. There are roughly 30 or so other guys here now, various nationalities. I'm quite chuffed as there are three other Brits and a Yank who have now joined the ranks. Each nationality generally sticks together; naturally the Yanks are accepted within the realms of the Brits and we quickly form a strong bond. The bond between the English-speaking peoples of the world is steadfast in itself but in the Legion I've found it the more so and envy from the others is ever present, with remarks often being made, but what of it? We are indeed a special breed; this bulldog pedigree is unique in many ways and none more so than among ex-pats.

Within a few days we were all kitted out with military denims and assembled on the parade square with our civvies tucked away in kit bags and suitcases. We were then put onto a coach and driven to the railway station in the centre of Paris, at the platform stood a long train awaiting our arrival; we were quickly ushered on board by our accompanying NCOs (*sous officiers*), who would make the ten-hour train journey to the south of France with us. Already great anticipation of where we were going took hold of my mind. The Yank came into my compartment carrying a case of beer in his large hands and grinning that he had found a bar on board the train, so most of the remainder of the journey to Marseilles was done behind the bottle.

At Marseilles, we changed trains to a town called Aubangne. This is where the *lière* Regiment étrangère was stationed (1st Foreign Regiment) and this is where all the processing of individuals is carried out in earnest, especially by the security staff who liaise with Interpol. It was not uncommon to see the police arrive and cart guys off to jail for some crime that they had not declared to the Legion and it served as a reminder to all to declare their past activities.

More medical checks are made together with educational examinations. That's right, even education is a priority in the Legion, and is carried out in all languages on the face of the planet. Our educational officer was also an American who, believe it or not, spoke at least ten other languages apart from his native tongue; now, who dare declare that the English-speaking race is lazy in adapting to new languages.

Career choices are available within the Legion together with what regiment you want to serve in, and provided you make the grade of graduating from boot camp and obtaining the coveted *Kepi Blanc* (White Cap), then the system and its officers will endeavour to fulfil the request of the individual.

But these are still early days and more weeks have to be spent in doing menial or worse tasks here in Aubangne. Even at this stage I was aware of the monastic life the Legion requires of its soldiers, and knew the truth of enlisting to forget. If you didn't then you would not survive the harsh training that lay ahead.

There are quite a lot of refugees in the Legion, in particular from such countries as the former Yugoslavia, both Croatia and Serbia, and from former eastern block countries, not to mention those from the Middle East and Asia. Perhaps the Legion, being so unique in its diversity, is able to fight in many theatres of war by having within its ranks such people as these, and perhaps this reason alone sets the Legion apart as one of the best special forces units operating around the world.

I had left home some three months before and had survived the waiting and processing stage of the Legion. We were then given another chance to leave, if we desired. None who had reached this far wanted to opt out and we were invited to sign the contract of the Legion. To serve with Honour and Fidelity (*avec Honeur et Fidelité*), to be terminated five years from hence if so desired, or to re-engage.

A group of 50 of us left the camp at Aubangne to be packed on to a train and this time to head westward in the direction of Carcassonne, to a place called Castelnaudary, not far from the foothills of the French Pyrenees. Unlike the camp at Aubangne, Castelnaudary was not unlike a real French Foreign Legion fort except for perhaps the lack of surrounding desert. This was replaced by rolling green fields and endless grapevines that seemed to go on in all directions as far as the eye could see. In this way it was different to camps I'd been to in the UK, in that in those were surrounded by training areas.

I was not disappointed; the whole functioning of the Legion and of its methods of rookie training were not unlike the British Army. The fields of pleasure as we Brits decided to name the training area were here after all, only about five or ten kilometres from camp but neatly camouflaged from the untrained eye but within easy reach of the recruit to visit at least twice a day.

Great physical emphasis is put on obtaining complete fitness within the Legion and second best will never do. If a member doesn't shape up quickly within the section then the section as a whole suffers. And although the sections have many international non-French-speaking soldiers, you soon get the message when you've pissed down the wrong leg of the officer in charge.

Of course there are many barriers to cross for the hopeful Legionnaire, the language being the main one. Failing to speak French and understand it brings with it many problems. Loneliness and feeling isolated from others present is the greatest danger, especially if you have none of your own nationals within your section. The Legion does recognise this

83

problem within the recruit training programme and does offer help by giving French lessons to those who do not speak the language. But like most things you soon learn to adapt and, if there was doubt that you would not make it, then the chances are that you would not have even got this far. It is up to you how quickly you learn and adapt. It does help if you forget your identity of belonging to a certain culture and try to focus on the task in front of you. And that is to be awarded the coveted *Kepi Blanc*.

I probably found the training pretty much the same as going through P company in the British Army, and knew what to expect from the instructors and what *hell* they can and will dish out at the slightest provocation, however trivial. I was probably fortunate in having another Brit and the Yank within my section, who like myself had previous military backgrounds to fall back on when times went bad or worse; I did see people break under the pressure of simply being unable to communicate and becoming isolated.

Almost our entire training was done in the Pyrenees, which offered us all some gruelling times, with long route marches to cover in only a short amount of time, but more often than not the spectacular sights that greeted you were enough to keep your mind off the hardships; and the sheer glory of having overcome the tasks in hand only added to the wonderful privilege of being a trainee Legionnaire.

This feeling was again captured at our presentation of the *Kepi Blanc*. After two months of training in basic elements of soldiering followed by a long march over five days, we rested up in one of the Legion's own farm buildings tucked away deep in the Pyrenees. Around about ten in the evening and after the autumn sun had reclined into the stillness of the night, we were gathered around the campfire that was burning brightly in the paddock area of the farm. There we began to sing the traditional Legion songs that we had learned and recited over the past few months as part of the training programme.

We were dressed in our combat gear but wore no beret as part of our dress, only the red and green epaulettes used for special occasions were worn on each of our shoulders to signify the awarding of the *Kepi*. Again we pledged allegiance to the Foreign Legion and stated that we had now put everything behind us in our past lives, and that now the Legion was indeed our country: *Legio Patria Nostra*.

We were awarded the *Kepi Blanc* and were allowed for the first time to drink alcohol and partake of the slaughtered lamb that was being roasted on the open fire. It reminded me of taking Holy Communion at a church and making a pledge to God, and was administered with almost the same reverence as a spiritual service.

This was not the end of basic training, rather another stage in the process, being allowed certain rewards in return for accomplishing an initial stage. For most of the guys the *Kepi Blanc* meant only one thing, *carte libre*, freedom to go out on the town and the Legion, like most other armies, lives on the reputation of its men being able to drink and I mean drink.

The next two months of training took two parallel routes. The first of these is an individual skill, the second, special tactical techniques. The vocational subjects are usually a foreign language, signalling or medicine, explosives or marksmanship etc. Whatever the Legion sees in your performance as an individual will be spotted by the instructors and, as time goes by during the training period, they may then suggest you move on to a more specialised programme to help develop your skill. After this has been acquired, group tactical skills are of importance, but these are usually put to one side until the individual reaches his regiment.

As was the case of myself, I was allocated for training with the 2nd Parachute Regiment based on the island of Corsica. The island is home to two of the Legion's and France's most potent special forces, one being the *2ième* REI, the other being the *2ième* REP. Both are in action more than any other unit within the French military system. This is where you learn the risk of becoming a Legionnaire often without any acknowledged glory. Many of the Legion's exploits have gone unnoticed by the majority of reporters throughout the world, simply because the sheer mention of the Foreign Legion is usually enough to end quite a lot of crises.

On the island things are done very differently within the Legion; there is no waiting about pussy-footing, the OC wants you up and running as soon as possible within the regiment and no time is wasted in getting you trained to operate within your section. This is where the tactical skills are learnt.

Remember this regiment is constantly ready to operate anywhere in the world at short notice. Its operation is not unlike the British SAS and other special service units which can work together closely and are often mutually involved in conflicts around the world. Perhaps the Legion has a more romantic tale to tell due to the many famous guests that have been absorbed into its ranks in the past, from kings to paupers, politicians to poets, murderers, molesters, thieves and liars. Whatever the world has created in man, the Legion has had at one time in its ranks and has successfully helped many to transform them into worthwhile men.

It became an interesting time to examine the different men that I served with. I wondered about the reasons why these men had volunteered; had they too struggled with their past lives? Had they wrestled their souls as I had done? Had they an inner desire to search for a better life than they had out in the world? Had they, like myself, been possessed with anger of misspent youth? Had they too joined to forget? Or was this such a time to do penance for the wrong that they had done. My mind explored the many reasons as to why so many men simply wander off to join the Legion.

Each had his own reason as I had mine. What is it that attracts all the world's misfits to this family of fighting men who, in the world's eyes, are common thugs, criminals, rejected by their fellowmen and country as undesirables and outcasts of society? Yet these men of untold shame would gladly sacrifice their lives in place of yours, and often do, for the sake of freedom that they themselves have never found among their own kin. For many the Legion is a sense of belonging and becomes itself a country to them. And, although the Legion has no home of its own, its men fight on not necessarily for higher ground but for a possible higher glory.

I had been with the Legion *2ième* REP for two and a half years and, although stationed at Calvi on the island of Corsica, we were very rarely back at camp. My tour had taken me to various parts of the world, from Chad to Djibouti patrolling the vast deserts of the Sahara in north Africa on the borders of Libya, to the battle-grounds of the Lebanon and Beirut in the Middle East. The French still have interests of their own throughout the world and the Legion is used to the full both by the French and her allies. There is a price of course to be paid to the French authorities, who in turn pay the wages of the Legionnaires. The Legion is part of the French Army otherwise we would have to be called a mercenary force, and the Legion dissociates itself from this concept of its function.

Usually, half way through your five-year engagement with the Legion, it is customary to be posted to another regiment somewhere else in the world. You can choose where to serve and provided there is a place your request is usually granted. Unlike the British Army the Legion is not restricted as to where it can send its soldiers. My request took me to the complete opposite side of the world to the great rain forests of South America. We flew in low over the jungle towards Cayenne military airport in French Guiana. Guiana had once been a French penal colony for its political and criminal offenders, and it seemed more than appropriate that the Legion was here. It had been indeed, since the end of the French Indo-Chinese war (Vietnam), where the Legion again bore the brunt of the fighting and was almost completely exterminated with overwhelming casualties.

Instantly I fell in love with this beautiful country. With its lush greenery and wildlife and its inhabitants, it was as if time had stood still until I arrived to look upon its delicate beauty and splendour and to acknowledge that there was someone out there in the vastness of our own space or inner imagination. A Creator of such magnitude and beauty that no word could express or comprehend. It was one of those moments when it is better to say nothing and enjoy the sheer delight of casting your eyes on beauty itself and letting beauty comfort your troubled soul. Being at one with the surroundings there is no need to find words.

Grabbing our gear we boarded the army trucks that were waiting outside the airport to take us to the HQ of the *3ième* REI based at Kourou some 30 or 40 kilometres from Cayenne. The journey was to last about an hour and I quickly made myself comfortable, with amazement relishing how this place looked.

As with life, beauty changes its face all too quickly; from tree-top level all appeared well from the aircraft. Not until we passed through some of the townships of the countryside did we see the poverty of many of its inhabitants, neglected by their government who opt to favour the wealthier nations in exploiting their resources. I could not help feeling for these people, perhaps because I too had once felt cheated by my government and people and neglected by what was once my family and friends.

The town of Kourou is heavily populated with Europeans, almost all employed by the European Space Centre only eight kilometres away. At least four times a year huge rockets are launched into space with various payloads ranging from communication satellites to experimental craft. One of the Legion's functions was to patrol and protect the Space Agency's interests in and around South America. We were lucky to be housed in one of the modern buildings around Kourou, a block of luxury apartments that was home to about 2,000 Legionnaires – only four guys to an apartment meant that privacy was easily come by. We were allowed to buy mod cons such as TVs and washing machines and to furnish the rooms as we wanted. It felt good to be able to live a little more like a human being and with a little more independence; it does wonders for the morale.

One of the things all the newcomers had to go through was to learn how to cross a fast-flowing river and be able to keep all their gear in their bergens dry. Most of Guiana is only accessible by rivers and swamps and learning how to keep things dry in the rain forest is an essential part of survival and played a large part in preventing all sorts of tropical diseases occurring. During our first two weeks we were taught the arts of jungle survival and warfare; the course was named 'Stage

Bruce', which conjured up pictures of it being organised by a wild Australian bushman from the outback. I guess he had long gone as our paths never crossed.

We were issued with specially made canvas bergens lined with plastic along with specially made jungle boots (*portuagas*). These were made from Gortex with rubber soles and were light and comfortable even on long patrols on the rivers. They were not suitable for long walks in the jungle; for this we were issued with two pairs of Rangers, normal army-issue leather and rubber type. A US Marines-issue hammock and, of course, the ever-faithful machete bush knife (made in England). A smaller knife was also supplied, a US Marines issue Camulus, worth its weight in gold and an essential tool never to be without. Other knick-knacks were provided but the most treasured possession was a simple plastic sheet no more than ten foot square which could be put to an array of assorted practical uses – when tied above your hammock between two trees it made life a little more comfortable when the rainy season took hold or, when you had to cross a deep river, you would wrap the bergen up inside the plastic sheet, tie it down well and float it across a river; not only did it keep your gear dry but it helped you keep afloat as the air inside the sheet was trapped.

Stage Bruce lasted for about ten days after which the newcomers were dispatched to their respective sections and duties. The *3ième* Regiment is basically an infantry regiment consisting of four companies each specialising in certain functions within the regiment's requirements. The *2ième* and the *3ième* companies specialised in all types of conflicts that arise in jungle warfare and are kept busy patrolling deep within the rain forests for long periods, months rather than weeks. It was usual for only one company at a time to be

Figure 1: 'G' squadron 22nd Independent Para Regt (Pathfinder). En route to aircraft at RAF Brize Norton.

Figure 2: A successful drop at sunset.

Figure 3: On parade at the legion depot (Quatier Lapasset) Castelnaudary, Southern France. Home to the 4em Regt Legion Etrangere. This is where every recruit is put through hell for four gruelling months of his basic legion training: only after his success is he deployed to specialist training with another regt somewhere in the domains of a hidden warfare around the globe.

Figure 4: 2em Regt Rep. Parachute Regt of the Foreign Legion: diving section
on patrol somewhere on the island of Corsica in the Med.

Figure 5: Prep. for a big drop! At Calvi, Corsica:
author shown on the right.

Figure 6: From right to left: Jock, myself, Porter, Greg; posing for the camera on arrival in French Guiana, South America, during our 3-year tour of duty.

Figure 7: A fire fight caught on camera within the canopy of the jungles of South America.

Figure 8: Part of the famous Devil's island: Royale and St Joseph.
Used for moments of recuperation by the Legion on return from long
missions within the jungle.

Figure 9: Jean (ox) Delmar and myself enjoying a glass of whisky
before returning to France 1982.

Figure 10: Within only a short while on arrival from South America, training begins on the snowy wastes of the French Alps.

The author today.

deployed on long-range penetration missions while the other would stay back at Kourou performing Legion tasks, such as patrolling the European Space Centre around the launch site or mounting the guard at one of the camps. Internally, each of the companies was made up of three or four sections consisting of roughly 30 men per section; within each section groups were formed consisting of about eight or ten men. Both the CE (*Compagnie Equipment*) and the CCS (*Compagnie Commandement du Service*, Company Command Service) which formed the remainder of the companies within the Legion were designated to do other tasks.

The CE specialised in building and road making and was currently undertaking the construction of a highway that would link French Guiana with its neighbours of Surinam and Brazil. They were based at Regina and were hoping to link up with the Brazilian route 156 at the Oiapoque river which separates Guiana from Brazil. These guys are out and about for many months at a time and only get back to Kourou three times a year when they perform normal soldiering duties with the exception of guard duties.

As well as being construction specialists and responsible for many difficult tasks, they are in their own right a specialised unit and many of the guys within the regiment who found it difficult to cope with the strain of going on long patrols with the other two fighting groups opted to being attached to the CE.

The CCS were responsible for the general running of things within the regiment, and for supply and resupply (Logistical Command and Support). On long patrols they were attached to the other groups at section level where they were responsible for arranging transport and medical teams etc. Incidentally, the Legion has a fantastic medical set-up and possesses within its ranks the best military doctors within any armed force; they accompany the units on all their missions.

At our disposal we also had two Transall aircraft, slightly smaller than the C130 Hercules but just as effective for dropping troops and supplies where needed in a hurry. Four Super Puma helicopters and two Gazelle attack helicopters were also permanently attached to the regiment.

After only about six weeks within my company my section was allocated to do a tour of duty patrolling some of the vast network of rivers that criss-crossed the entire region of Guiana: Mission Trois Sauts. We were given about a week to prepare for the mission and to get all our equipment together for this tour, which was to last six to eight weeks. It was like embarking on some form of expedition, everything had to be labelled, checked, relabelled and rechecked before it was entered into the section Levi as being complete and then packed into large waterproof sacks and again labelled and stored ready to be put on the convoy of trucks that was to transport us to the military air base at Cayenne (Remire).

It took the best part of the day to load the trucks – as soon as one was finished another would arrive to be loaded. At least two trucks were needed to transport ten Johnson outboard motors together with the eight large barrels of fuel that would keep them running for the duration of our mission. Each engine had attached to it a hundred feet of rope, at the end of which was a fluorescent buoy in case any accidents should occur on the river and somebody should fall from the pirogues (dug-outs).

Another truck was allocated to transport the explosives and ammunition that were required. This included a large number of Winchester pump action shot-guns carefully oiled and cased into wooden crates for transportation. In total some eight trucks were needed to transport all the equipment and men that were to embark on the mission.

We arrived in the early hours of the afternoon at the air base and after a brief lunch we were deployed to load the large transporter aircraft, carefully directed by the air force load-master. Everything was secured and large nets were placed over the munitions. This was made easier by being able to drive the trucks inside the plane before being unloaded; it became unbelievably hot and we were only allowed to work for short periods at a time inside the aircraft, alternating in shifts.

Everything secure, the two enormous engines roared into life and the air-conditioning began to function in the hold where we were squeezed among the stores. The flight lasted for about an hour.

St Georges was only equipped with a rough landing strip carved out of the jungle on the northern borders of the Brazilian jungle. The plane circled a couple of times before making a steep final approach to the air strip and, after a bumpy landing, we were safely back on terra firma. The huge exit doors at the rear of the aircraft opened and we were greeted by the native residents of St Georges, who were all friendly and beaming. To my amazement they helped in unloading the aircraft and carrying the equipment down towards the quayside of the river Oyapok (Oiapoqu) which divided the two countries from one another. A skeleton crew was left there with a senior NCO while the rest of us walked to a small outpost that could house up to 40 men quite comfortably.

We stayed at St Georges for only about three days as we got things together and divided the equipment on to the six pirogues each about 30 feet long, especially made to the

Legion's requirements. Although they were long they were very narrow and shallow in depth, but it was unbelievable what would fit into these boats. A powerful outboard motor on the stern made them very effective for patrolling the rivers. Each boat had two Indians positioned at either end, who knew all the rivers without ever having to consult a map or compass and who made fantastic guides and trackers for the Legion's missions within the jungle. They were skilled hunters for food, as we would soon find out.

Our first objective was to reach a small Indian village called Camopi some 100 kilometres south of St Georges; that took about two and a half days on the river. It was absolutely fantastic and beyond anything that I'd previously experienced; although the rainy season had passed we were still experiencing a few heavy showers and were often kept busy bailing water from the boats. After each shower had passed it became twice as hot and humid as water evaporated from the forest and the river; banks of mist would suddenly appear and the convoy would have to pull in to the side and await its dispersal for an hour or so before we could continue.

We made camp each evening at around five p.m., near the river bank. Putting up your hammock and plastic could be done in a few minutes, then we would split into small groups, one to forage for firewood, another to dig urinals, another to build a kitchen complete with table and benches. Within two hours we would all be sitting around a campfire enjoying our first hot meal of the day and chatting to one another over the past day's activities on the river.

It was quite safe to have a high profile at this stage of the mission towards Camopi, and we were allowed to take things easy and to enjoy the magical mystery tour along the river. It felt like a pleasure cruise at times and the beauty of this land became a spiritual experience in its own right; seeing all sorts of wildlife in its natural habitat gave endless wonder of what this sacred world held.

At Camopi we were greeted by the local tribal chief and were given permission to eat with the villagers, a meal of anaconda and cayman meat, my first experience of eating exotic food, which gave me the shits for days afterwards. Tokens of goodwill were exchanged by the officer in charge who gave the chief a large bag of pure cooking salt in exchange for a multitude of local gifts like hunting spears and carved effigies.

The story has it that Indians will give you anything for salt, even their women; perhaps this is why we were not going to stay at the village overnight. Our camp lay over 200 metres away over the other side of the cayman-infested river and none of us ventured out to cross it, not even to take advantage of such a prospect. I spent the evening listening to the sounds of the jungle that by now had awoken, to all sorts of strange sounds that haunted the black night beneath the forest canopy. At times throughout the night I was awakened by the snarl of mosquitoes around my mosquito net, determined to gain entry. A small tear in it ensured I did not have an easy night.

We were all up before sunrise, drinking hot coffee around the campfire that had been kept alight during the night by the section who mounted the guard, and eating a breakfast that consisted of dry biscuits and strawberry jam. As the sun rose higher and daylight pierced the canopy, clearing the ground mist from the bush below, we broke camp ready to embark. The Indian guides were already bailing out the pirogues as we made our way down to the shore, as usual grinning at everyone as we cautiously stepped on to the boats.

Our next port of call was Oscar, some 75 kilometres away as the crow flies but rivers are very seldom straight so we had getting on for a 100 to do. The river was running high after the rainy season and navigation was becoming difficult even for the Indians; water was coming from everywhere and with it extra danger; debris was also a hazard and hitting a tree in the middle of a fast-flowing river could mean instant disaster. It was suggested that everyone should don life jackets and hold on for dear life.

It was like riding white rapids all the way down to Oscar. Huge waves engulfed the boats and everyone was kept busy trying to keep the water level down using anything that could contain water. No sooner had you emptied some of the water out than another wave came swamping the boats once again; we were kept busy constantly trying to keep the boats from capsizing for at least six hours – not a moment's rest all day. It reminded me of my days on the trawlers and of the ferociousness of the seas, and man wrestling with the elements. I never even thought of the caymans, anacondas and piranha living in the river – we just concerned ourselves with emptying the boat of the water.

We decided to make camp early that day, cleaned up some of the mess in the boats and changed one of the outboard motors that had suffered some damage to its propeller shaft when it struck a rock. The next day the river had subsided somewhat and, instead of a murky brown like liquid chocolate, it was clear. The sun was coming through the river mist and it looked as if we would be able to make a good headway down to Oscar. We filled all the petrol tanks and also decided, to save time on stopping half way down to refuel, to fill all the reserve tanks and change them as we went along. Full throttle all the way, it was good to be back to normal and to enjoy the pleasant surroundings and watch the abundant wildlife perform daily rituals of survival. We arrived at the village of Oscar shortly before dusk and quickly made camp and got a fire on the go so we could cook some hot food and a cuppa. We carried some fresh food on the way but most of the time we saved it until the evening *repas* where we could prepare it and enjoy it at its best with a bottle of wine beside a campfire. It was also the first time that we could bathe properly and wash some of the stench out of our clothes; it was all fine until one of the guys came across a gigantic anaconda and proceeded to attack the creature with a machete cutting it into several pieces. We all got out of the river, slowly enough not to reveal that we were fearful of what else lay within the hidden depths; but no one appeared to hang around in the water too long after that.

The next day we radioed HQ back at Kourou for the latest news and orders. The Legion patrols the northern borders with Brazil taking care that no illegal contraband is smuggled through between Brazil and Surinam to the east of French Guiana; arms and drugs are big business, together with illegal gold mining.

All was reported quiet on the borders and, according to the heli report, there was no unusual activity in the area. This was a good time to practise a few tactical manoeuvres and the OC ordered that from now on we did everything by the book. That was a signal to us that the relax-max attitude was over for us for a while at least.

We were issued with extra live ammunition and fragmentation grenades together with the Winchester pump shot-guns. These were a favourite with most of us and were ideal for clearing the bush in close-quarter skirmishes. Light body armour was also essential (flak jackets) but seemed to weigh

a ton by the end of the day. Throughout the day we prac-
tised the buddy-buddy system within the section and also
sequence search-and-destroy methods that would be employed
if required.

The following day was significant in that everyone's mood
had changed from the happy-go-lucky to become more serious
and purposeful, as we thought of what might be in store for us
along the way. I made sure that all my weapons were close to
my side and were within easy reach.

The way down towards Trois Sauts was going to be different
from the rest of the journey as we were all on a state of
alert and anticipated trouble. Cache Manana is roughly 80
kilometres away from Oscar and a lot of 'trade' comes from
the Brazilian inlets and rivers especially from the river
Murare: most of the contraband starts from the town of
Macapa, brought in by plane or ship from various other
parts of the world; from there it is usually put on to a truck
and driven a 100 kilometres north using route 156 to Porto
Grande. Then it is put on to boats and distributed to various
places in the network of the hundreds of small rivers along the
border of French Guiana. Our purpose was to intercept this
illegal trade.

Two days further on and we had had no contact with any
smugglers. We were even sent on small patrols within the
interior in the hope of finding some recent evidence of any
intrusion or camp that had recently been abandoned, again no
luck. We made contact with a reconnaissance helicopter who
had reported seeing something suspicious some ten kilometres
further down from our position. My immediate thought was of
the French tendency to be suspicious of everything and to be
easily excitable; I dismissed the danger.

Our boat took the lead. The first sign of trouble was when

the Indian guide who stood at the stern of the boat was hit. The other boats took evasive action, trying to reposition themselves to return fire. Meanwhile our helmsman was going completely bonkers and, screaming with anger, having seen where the shots were coming from, he sped at full throttle towards the bank.

By now we were all taking cover as well as we could. One of the guys opened up with a long blast from a AA52 machine gun in the direction of the rifle shots as another pulled the injured Indian down into the boat and covered his wounds with a field dressing. The helmsman, still intent on getting the pirogue closer to the action, headed flat out towards it. The rest of us anticipated what was going to happen next and quickly jumped overboard before the boat stuck nose first into the bank, discharging some of the baggage as well as the injured Indian who was now lying on the grass groaning in agony. We secured the area as best we could and tried to locate the enemy, but since we had beached there was only silence apart from the screeching of birds startled by the gunfire.

We lay among the undergrowth for what seemed like eternity, but in reality only a few minutes before we let rip with a few close quarter rounds from the Winchester, as three other bods searched the surrounds and established an OP on our flanks and ahead. We then called for reinforcements to be dropped off along the river banks by the others at intervals of 25 metres or so and to blockade passing traffic on the river in case they chose to make a run for it. Again firing, this time to the right of me but some distance away and then a sudden fire fight erupted with all sorts of weapons being used.

It was a brief encounter but a lesson to those who want to

engage the Legion in combat. It was decided after a clean-up that a small group would head deep into the forest to see if there was anything else that we had missed or should know about, and then would rendezvous with us down stream some 15 kilometres away. The rest of us took an easier route on the river to Trois Sauts, stopping regularly to put a small recce party ashore to survey the area. It was decided also that on reaching Trois Sauts and in view of what had taken place, the main contingent would disembark and make a patrol of some 30 kilometres west toward Degrad Haut Camopi while a skeleton section would bring the boats through the shallow waters and rapids and link up with the main detachment somewhere on the river Camopi. First we had to strip the boats clear of most of the baggage, apart from the really heavy stuff that was made doubly secure and tied down and left inside the boat.

The slow march took about two and a half days to complete through swamps infested with mosquitoes and blood-sucking leeches and most of the way had to be cut away by using our machetes. Another small group was detailed to reconnoitre ahead as the forest became more and more dense.

Our first night out on patrol was spent in the swamps and flooded riverside. We found no dry ground to make any encampment that evening so we had to mount our hammocks above the waist-deep water on the branches of the trees; all the equipment had to be firmly attached to a secure point within easy reach in case of an emergency during the night. The night was hell and it was only possible to doze off from time to time however tired one was. The mosquitoes are something else out there and can drive you completely mad; I've quite honestly been able to wipe my hand over my face and collect sufficient mozzies to be able to make a good size ball and roll them out of the palm of my hand on to the floor below – it has been that bad.

If that wasn't enough at odd times during the night I was awakened by the sounds of hammocks falling into the water. This sounds funny I know, and I must admit I did laugh until I too fell. It was hopeless to rest in this situation and most of us kept awake afraid that if anyone was to attack us now, then they would have a field day at our expense – we were vulnerable not only to the natural elements but to an enemy who for all we knew possessed modern night vision equipment and could be watching our free comedy act trying to keep dry and sane within this hell-hole. Thankfully the crocs stayed away at least.

We couldn't do anything until sunrise the following day, forget the coffee get the f*** out of the swamp as quickly as possible to our rendezvous for that evening. I was knackered and almost collapsed with exhaustion while putting up my hammock, but I resisted the temptation to climb straight into it. I had a good wash in a pool and then something hot to eat and drink and maybe a nip of brandy.

I slept well that night until I was awakened by someone who told me it was my turn to mount a two-hour guard. Have you ever thought of going home? Or wondering what the hell you were doing out here? This was one of those times when you are awakened in the middle of the night and you don't want to get out of your pit. I cursed for having been disturbed but eventually crawled out of my hammock to mount the watch.

The moon was bright enough to pierce through the towering trees and offered a comforting light as I went about my duties checking that all was secure about the camp. After a while I deposited my rear end on a log that was conveniently placed overlooking the shallow pool that I'd bathed in. The moon reflecting in the water made me think of back home and suddenly my eyes were full of tears.

Sitting on that log in the middle of a South American forest I wept like a child. It gave me comfort just to weep and be all alone with my past memories and with nature. What was I trying to accomplish by being in the Legion? I could not answer myself and gave one last deep breath in an attempt to regain my composure and to hold on to my manhood. Time to get off the log and go about my duties, to keep my mind off the past – I didn't regret joining the Legion, only what had brought me to it.

The remainder of the patrol was completed with no more incidents and we finally got back to St Georges after six weeks, a little thinner around the waist but more aware of the harsh environment of the jungle and how to cope in it.

Back at Kourou we had a week of cleaning all the material and frequenting the local brothel organised by the Legion and conveniently placed within walking distance of the camp. The *pouffe*, as the Legion called the brothel, was a grotty hut built of breeze blocks and corrugated tin sheets, and housed a small selection of women who would satisfy these lusty soldiers of fortune. For 50 francs you got yourselves a South American ride. You might have to wait a while and be last in the queue but who's bothered? Credit is available at the bar as you wait your turn and you can drink as much as you want. Or you can try your luck in the shanty town a few kilometres away but all you will find is the same women that were in the *pouffe* the previous month. (Almost all the women that offer a service are rotated every four weeks or so by the organisers to offer some variety for the clients.)

Within ten days of arriving back at camp we were packed

and ready for some R and R (Rest and Recuperation). We were packed on to a landing craft in Kourou harbour early in the morning along with provisions and a generous amount of wine and beer to last for several days. Our heading was about 20 kilometres out to sea, a small group of three islands commonly called Iles du Salût – St Joseph, Le Royale and Diable, Devil's Island. The Legion has a rest camp on St Joseph. It was fantastic to be able to relax on this small paradise island beneath the palm trees and to be isolated and surrounded by the ocean with no snakes; and even better, no mosquitoes to worry about. It was a time to recuperate and catch up on some of the sleep we had lost during the mission and to put all our bad and negative thoughts behind us. Time was spent on leisurely activities and having some fun together as a group. It served a purpose of getting to know each other on a more personal basis especially the new guys who had just arrived.

Among these were three guys from the UK who were placed in my section. Within hours of their arrival and introduction the *Mafia Anglais* became well known within the section. For me it was a godsend that at last I could relate to people in my own native tongue again and share both deep thoughts as well enjoying the British humour that I had missed. And what a place to get to know one another out here on this island with a bottle of wine at hand. I entertained them with frightening stories of the jungle, of course it was all bull but they bought it!

Most of the time I spent in the Legion was spent doing what soldiers do mostly when not at war – training, endless training, but with a difference. We were sent to the Caribbean islands of Martinique and Guadalupe three times during training programmes of various sorts: commando training, airborne intervention and rescue missions were always a top priority and whenever we were not out on a live mission somewhere in the jungles of the Americas then we would be dispatched somewhere exotic on manoeuvres.

Back to camp for a few weeks and the whole process began again: another mission, another objective. There was no time to get bored, there was always something going on. That's not to say that the individual had no free time of his own; like most armies, we had paid leave of six weeks a year and were given the opportunity to visit other lands (friendly) within the Americas. On some vacations it was possible to hitch a free flight from the French Air Force who flew regularly to the French colonies in the Caribbean and, provided that there was room on the aircraft, you could get there and back for free.

While in Guiana I was promoted to corporal chef, the equivalent of sergeant, and was given more responsibility (mostly for all the things that went wrong). Life was then a little easier to cope with; after all you got other people to do a lot of the ordinary work. Each month brought with it new guys to the regiment – they seemed to be getting younger each month – and the English-speaking community had grown to around 30 or so guys. A couple of the lads had even brought with them their wives – you can get married within the Legion and have married quarters to live in, provided you have served over five years and have reached the rank of corporal chef and have then become a French national (an option given to all serving members of the Legion with five years' service).

I had by now been in the Legion for four and a half years and out here in the hot humidity of the jungles I had changed from being a thug and a crook into something more accept- able to society. These last remaining months I had left out here would be spent on a little soul searching asking myself the many questions I had long since forgotten.

Is this the life for me? Although I enjoyed army life it wasn't for being gung-ho, or even for pride that I was a member of this most special force, to boast to others that I was there and relish the memories, becoming some kind of hero. There was, I think, a much deeper reason for becoming a member of the Legion.

The Legion served the purpose of making me see things rather differently. As a soldier I was exposed to many dangers in less than hospitable circumstances, and yet there were other experiences, memories of overwhelming peace and beauty. The memories are left deep within my soul of how things were in my life, and of how I had to struggle to overcome the bitterness that had grown in my heart, of coming to realise where I was going in life. One day I felt the strength to take on all adversaries, the next I became burden-some to myself and wanted to give. But what mattered most was that each new day I stood up to the wind and tried, and in this I found the profound meaning of the Legion motto 'March or Die'.

7

Another Place, Another Time

Frankly, I was in two minds as to whether or not to make a further commitment to the Legion and not bother going back home to the UK. But for the love of my family I would have stayed put. I felt it had been long enough without seeing them or hearing from them apart from the odd letter sent to my sister Sue. Time had dissolved a lot of my bitterness and selfish contempt and I felt more of a worthy fellow to face my family and friends again.

Was I ready to face them again? I still had doubts whether or not they cared any more. Few of them replied to my letters, which made things seem worse than they probably were: but what of it? I had to make the first move.

I travelled from the south of France with another Brit, who, like myself, had similar reasons to go home and confront his past and his family. We passed the time with reflections on the journey we had made some five years ago when a whole new world was awaiting us with open arms and we were about to enlist. Now we were going back to our old world and our past with some trepidation.

I telephoned my sister from London's Euston station and told her I was back home in the UK. I didn't say much else as I was waiting to hear her response, and sure enough, without thinking twice she invited me to stay with her for a while. At least one member of the family still cared. We greeted one another as brother and sister do and I was introduced to her family. 'Struth, had it really been this long since I had seen them? Over dinner I was made to talk about my adventures in the Legion and felt at last some pride in what I had done.

I hadn't the heart to tell her that I hadn't yet decided whether to re-enlist. I knew I could still go back within three months, and for now I decided to tell them that I was only on leave – it would save a lot of explaining as to what I was going to do with my life out in civvy street. And I had no plans as yet.

The second day I spoke to my sister Tina, but predictably it became an overwhelming emotional experience and I decided not to go and see her for fear of it disturbing her.

Out with my old chums, down the pub. Yes, it was still the same old life they were leading. Booze, drugs and petty chitchat, bragging to one another; what idiots they were, living the lives of never-beens. They knew nothing and wanted everything to fall at their feet. At times I felt like a fool; they tried to make me a laughing stock for having joined the Foreign Legion. Had I wanted to go back to my old self I would have broken something over their stupid heads – to me there was much more to life than hanging around street corners trying every angle to beat the system. I had had enough of them; their squalor and narrow-mindedness had only one effect on me, and that was to get the hell away from them and leave them to it.

107

I made my mind up to go back and re-enlist; there seemed no reason to have come back to the UK. I felt cheated a little, but I said all my farewells to family and friends giving them no indication of what I was going to do. I left my home town for what I hoped would be the last time.

I still had money in my pocket and decided to make a slow move down to Dover docks, stopping on the way down at a few hotels and spending most of the time in the bars hoping to pick up some easy woman for the night. My mind was becoming polluted with idle thoughts and again I was indecisive as to what I really wanted in life. I spent the first night alone, long and disturbed, wrestling with tormenting thoughts that drained me of energy.

The next day was no different. I drank more whisky and again had no luck in picking up a woman for the night. Perhaps it was the drink that was making me feel so restless in life again? I needed a woman to hold and to hold closely. I think I finally fell asleep in the early hours of the morning, pleading inwardly for some miracle to put me back on course as to what to do. Part of me wanted to go back to the Legion but a bigger part of me wanted to hold on for a while and stay. Frankly, I was tired of all that I had done with the Legion, but where else could I call home?

It was decided then. I would book in at a cheap B and B in Folkestone for three days and leave for France on the Wednesday. I still had my return ticket for the ferry crossing which was valid for another week and had sufficient funds to live on until then. At least it gave me the opportunity to clear my head a little.

Within hours my life was to change dramatically, a turning point that I did not even recognise at the time and only now, after some 15 years down the line of life to this present day, am I able in part to comprehend – of the majesty of a greater force at work than I ever could have imagined. Luck, coincidence? Destiny? I think not; time has made me feel more sure of myself in declaring that whatever you wish to call it, I call it God.

I've been physically and mentally laid to rest by a supreme power that I can no longer doubt watches over each of us, able to transform an untameable caged tiger such as I was. His methods vary, his tools are many, his strategy is hidden. Have I been led in this life down a path of endless heartaches to bring me to where I ought to be?

> Of troubled torment and fear of my soul.
> And for what greater purpose hath thee in mind?
> Of all the suffering, of all mankind.
> My ways have been broken, my life exposed
> to what end wilt thou hunt me O Lord?
> Thy will or mine?
> I have rested and have been restored
> No more looking back at Sodom or Gomorrah
> nothing now there, but stone
> I will serve.

I met her at the Café Royale. Over lunch she caught my eye from a table opposite and we exchanged smiles. I thought nothing of it at the time, just a glance and a friendly smile. In the B and B I offered to do a job or two, mainly to keep myself from getting bored and just to help pass the day away from doing nothing or ending up in a bar.

It was after lunch that the landlady asked me to help another resident to put the trash bins from the rooms outside the house ready for the refuse collection later that day. We knocked on the door of one and she stood there in front of me, red shoulder-length hair catching the mid-afternoon sun that was shining through the window. In what I first thought was a South African accent but then realised was Dutch she asked, 'You want koffee?'

We sat there, the three of us making simple conversation over hot coffee. We seemed to share a ready mutual understanding, although there was little to indicate that there was already a growing attraction between us. My mate had already finished his mug and was eager to return to work; she on the other hand insisted I stayed to finish my newly refilled mug and talk some more. Now 15 years later we are still holding the conversation, married with three children and living in a small village in the Dutch countryside. From when we first met and until this present day, she keeps me on course, sure and steadfast, always there beside me when I need her and always there it seems when I fall. And along with God she has given me my deeper thirst for life, and though I have given less than a promise, they have been more generous to me.

What greater gift to a man than that which turns all his life into a fountain? It was your loving mindfulness of my troubled days and tormented nights that have now made the food of life sweet to my mouth and girdled my sleep with visions of yet better times to come.

My life has changed over the years and not through some magical or mysterious spiritual experience, that many religions design to suit their own needs but do nothing but confuse the souls and minds of men. My experience has been of life, and of simple day-to-day survival, holding on to the belief in a creator and knowing him differently each day.

Within months I was reconciled with my family and made

110

peace with my father whom I loved dearly before he passed away. I still regret that I never got around to telling my mother I loved her also before she was taken.

Looking back on most of my life and reflecting on my somewhat checkered career I can now declare not only to others, but more importantly to myself, that wherever my troubled path led me in life I am now the richer, in character and in understanding. What I have, though, I haven't earned, for my reward is greater than the suffering. I have walked up a hill and come down a mountain.

My story does not explain why things happened as they did, that I deliberately stepped into a dark path which brought me into a constant confrontation with my soul and with society.

What it may do, perhaps, is give hope to others, those who like me have found themselves at odds with society and the law. They long for goodness and peace but life often treats them cruelly. Once it has struck its blows the wounds are deep, and once knocked off course it may take the rest of a life to find a new direction and a new wind to fill your sails. There are many more knocks to take and false paths to follow, but the falsest path is to accept failure and do nothing about it. You will only succeed in drifting into more troubled waters. Look deep within and take account of what you have and use it to your advantage. Never rest until you can feel a new breeze.

I felt a new wind.

Where it may lead me, who knows?

8

Family Ties

We lived for a short while in a one-room apartment, Anja and her two children (by her first marriage) and myself. It was a dirty, smelly place that overlooked the past grandeur of England's former wealthy architecture many years ago ... but this place was almost derelict and was badly in need of some repair. We didn't complain though ... at least we would be together and it offered us some security however it may have appeared to others. Even with all its faults, on reflection many years after some of our most happy memories together are from this shabby part of town. And, of course, this is where another part of my life was to begin albeit unclear as to what the future might hold, but I was very determined to succeed in any small way I could.

Regular work was, as always, upon my mind. Since leaving the military realms, I was now face to face with the reality of my situation and the state of our accommodation as a family. Often I would reflect on the times I had spent alone on the streets as a down and out before joining the Legion and remembered all too quickly of how so very easy it would be to get involved again with the criminal fraternity if things were to become desperate. And believe me ... things were becoming rapidly desperate; especially now that I had, almost overnight, gained an instant family.

Really, if it was not for my lovable landlady, who gave me some casual work to do that helped us overcome some of our financial predicaments, I don't know where things would have ended. Relying on welfare cheques and trying to manage to eat all the week as a family was difficult enough. Things went from bad to worse. And on one occasion I had to sell my military medals to a pawnbroker – five years' service and a small collection of campaign medals were sold for the grand sum of £45. A soldier's lot ... Some months later I tried to buy them back but unfortunately the shop no longer traded.

Enough time had been spent on writing applications for various jobs and a change of accommodation within the Folkestone region without any success. Things had become that bad that I wrote to my home town. A last resort in trying to climb the social ladder. But, as luck would have it, a reply was sent to us, offering a newly built house for us to lease.

I was a little uneasy at moving back to my home town for obvious reasons. The past has always haunted me about the place, as being somewhat unlucky for me. But all of my fears had to be somewhat kept a secret from my newly acquired family. If they knew of my criminal past then perhaps they too would reject me, regardless of my feelings. I knew how desperately Anja wanted us to have a proper home and seeing her face light up as we went to view the property only reaffirmed the decision I had to make.

Back in Folkestone, it didn't take too long to organise our

move north. And with the help of my trusted mate Chris, we packed our belongings and ourselves into his ageing jalopy of a car and headed home.

I think that both of us were subdued somewhat at leaving Folkestone and, while it didn't offer us much of a promise of better things to come in the way of opportunity, it certainly gave us our happiness together. Even without much money or a suitable home, enjoying the fruitiness of newly found love was a great blessing.

Our new home in Wellingborough came with newly acquired furniture, mostly donations from friends, whom I thought may have otherwise disposed of their items on the local council tip, but were essential to us in decorating our home. Anything and everything was welcomed and was put to some use, even an old bed on wheels (must have been from someone's grandparents) gave us and others it seems great pleasure, especially during passionate times. On several occasions we were cheered from an outside audience who had gathered beneath the bedroom window (mostly friends and neighbours) to listen to our memorable sessions on this particular bed. The thing was that we had no carpet on the bedroom floor. And each time we moved the slightest degree upon the bed, it would roll about the bedroom on its wheels, banging on the walls and other obstructions about the room. I think that it had an uneven wheel or something and this was not due to my performance in bed.

Another item, a settee, and given I think by the same mate, had obviously been given the same initiation tests over the years as the bed on wheels. For, if any romance was to be held upon it or anything other than its proper use, it would collapse into three parts (we only tried it once).

By now I was averaging two or three interviews a week, but

114

gaining employment was proving to be difficult to say the least and feeling excited in a new relationship was soon to be replaced with anxiety about the future. It was made worse by my past reputation and the high profile that the local press had given me some years before. Always people seemed to remember the things I'd done and judged me with the same contempt. Whatever, I still had not the heart to disclose my past life to Anja. The risk was just too great for me to take at the time.

It often became embarrassing to be stopped in the street by the local police when out and about and being asked, 'What are you doing back in town?' And always Anja would inquire. 'What did they want?' My reply was always well construed: 'They were just being friendly, darling, and asking if every-thing was well.'

I was really getting pissed off with the whole situation and decided that I had to begin with disclosing some of my past with her ... at least then she would understand why it was so difficult for me to find work.

As expected, being honest about my shady past didn't go down too well and I can only imagine what she thought of me at that particular time.

The heat really felt on now and, although I shared some of my hideous past with her, I felt even more under pressure to try to obtain some kind of work.

Weeks seemed to go by, and inside myself I was pleading with God for help. Again it seemed as if no answer came.

In the end I thought, Bugger everyone ... I borrowed some old heavy wooden ladders and went knocking on doors, asking people if they wanted their windows cleaned.

It was to my surprise that work became abundant almost overnight and after only a week I decided to have some printed leaflets dropped through the letter boxes. Pressure was almost instantaneously lifted by having some money in my pocket. And having some work to do made me feel a lot better and worthy.

It was very hard work and I was glad of an old schoolfriend to help carry the load around. Sometimes we would have to walk five miles over the fields to another village, carrying heavy ladders and equipment over our backs, just so we could earn a little extra cash. I thought I was at least blessed with having someone to help and who seemed as frustrated as I had been in my struggle to find work and who willingly walked across the long fields with me, to at least try to better himself in not relying on a welfare cheque each week. He managed only a few weeks with me however as he was not satisfied with his earnings at the end of his day.

After a couple of months I managed to buy a cheap car: to help with the heavy loads and to ease the long distances in walking in all manner of weather. I also had the odd helper but they never seemed to like the hard work or even sharing some of the cost involved, so they tended not to stick around too long. And the newly acquired car was proving to be disastrous and an even bigger mistake financially, besides making an unearthly noise. It discharged huge plumes of black smoke from its rear end; it was only running eight miles to the gallon of petrol. It was all proving to be a non-viable venture and within four months or so I was signing back on the dole.

The welfare system took its toll on the family again, with no help from them financially for over three weeks. We relied it seems on family and friends yet again. Somehow I just couldn't break away from this welfare system. No matter how much I tried I found myself in many Catch 22 situations with them. What made it harder for me was that I had a criminal record to contend with every time I wanted work. And you can guess for yourselves what the outcome was on every job interview.

To make matters worse, my time spent in the legion didn't help matters. It only served to arouse people's suspicion of my past in even greater depth. Now I was being branded not only a criminal but also a mercenary. I felt I was being put on show and somehow being made fun of by others who knew nothing of me and for whom I really was and strived so damn hard to become over these past years of my troubled life.

As if this wasn't enough to deal with, I now had the immigration people on my back concerning Anja and her children. They had given her 28 days to leave the country and to return to the Netherlands.

There was nothing else for it. We applied for a marriage licence and were married within three weeks. At least now the welfare state would have to give us more money now that we were a family. For six months we had survived on only an allowance given to a single person. Now we were entitled to a wider variety of claims, easing the situation.

While on our honeymoon (of sorts) and back in Folkestone I managed to get a regular job. An old acquaintance had suddenly propositioned full-time work, providing I could paint, that is. And of course I could. I had followed a painter/ decorator's course while serving time in one of Her Majesty's Prisons many years before. I didn't tell him though where I'd served my apprenticeship for a very good reason.

It was good to be back in Folkestone and our long weekend passed with the hope at long last that we could expect to achieve at least some of the little expectations of life itself.

The long drive back to Wellingborough was hurried. I almost had to leave straight away on the next train out of

117

town in order that I could start work in a couple of day's time. So, being completely being kitted out with some overalls and some rather iffy paint brushes and equipment, I departed from the station and my newly wedded wife and family.

I remember praying to myself for almost the entire journey south, asking and hoping things would turn out all right for us. I knew that if I remained in Wellingborough for much longer, that would be the end of everything for me. It would only be a matter of time before I fell into the bottomless pit of criminality again.

My first assignment on the job was an older-type semi-detached council house situated on an army camp, of all places, in a small place called Lydd on the Romney Marsh in Kent. Bill, my mate, made sure he looked after me and supplied me with endless help in making sure I'd done a good job on painting the external fixtures of the house. After all, it would come under criticism from the watchful eye of the contractor at the end of the week.

At first it was hard going. Most of the other guys achieved three to four houses by the end of the week and for me to accomplish one in only four days took some doing. But eh! I was new to the job and wanted to do this right. It paid off. Come Friday midday, the site manager appeared on the scene. He took a long time to inspect this freshly painted place. Already my arse cheeks were clenched firmly together, waiting to hear the words, 'you're sacked'. Instead, I could have kissed his arse. He actually congratulated me on doing such a grand job. And paid me £300. I was well happy and rushed to telephone Anja about my new success.

I carried on for a few more weeks before venturing back to visit Anja. And each week I was beginning to get better and quicker in finishing more houses and earning more money. It really felt good to be able to work and it boosted my self-esteem in every possible way.

Within a month I had enough money to put down a deposit on a furnished bungalow on the seafront in a place called Dymchurch. It was fantastic and I knew that Anja and the children would love it.

I telephoned when everything was arranged and simply said pack everything into boxes. I arrived on the following Friday night and by the Saturday afternoon we had packed everything into a small car I had purchased and were on our way back to Folkestone. We didn't even have time to say farewell to many of those who had helped us in all these dramatic months.

I just wanted to get away from everything and start a new life.

Her eyes sparkled! And tears of long-awaited joy began to roll down her cheeks when she set her sight on her new home. She could not believe it – this place was absolutely paradise.

We spent the most wonderful summer ever at this place and began to climb the social ladder towards better things. Winter, on the other hand was another story ... and the winter of 1984–5 was an unusual one. Even the sea was beginning to freeze over between France and the UK. A Siberian cold front had held most of the entire population on the south coast of Kent hostage with ferocious snow and ice storms covering the whole area with thick snow drifts and ice. We were all housebound for weeks on end and quite unable to go to work due to the bad weather. In the end we had to be laid off any construction work until the weather subdued.

This was not good news for us as, yet again, we had to approach the dreaded social system for help until the weather broke.

119

Eventually, spring did come and I got back to work as painter/decorator, although it took a few weeks before regular contracts were handed out to us and we could feel secure enough for the remainder of that year.

Anja had also started work as a private nurse (something which she is completely dedicated to) now that her English language was quite superior to mine: in fact, we were really well off financially and gradually we were replacing all of our old things about the house, for new.

We were even thinking of purchasing our own home, now that we were on our way up the ladder. After many months of searching for a suitable home, we decided to buy a house in Folkestone. It was hard to imagine that less than two years previously, we were more or less destitute and had no real aspirations in life. We certainly could never have envisaged buying our own home together, that's for sure. All seemed well at that stage in our lives and for the remainder of that year we spent most of our newfound wealth on modernising our new home, that is, until the following winter came.

You would have thought that we would have prepared ourselves better financially and have put some money away, at least to cover ourselves in case the work stopped as it had the previous winter. Me of all people should have thought about it long ago. Most of my work was within the building/construction trade and was always subject to the weather: the reason being most of the work involved was exterior work. Anyway, the winter came and again it hit us hard.

As in the past year, I was laid off for the duration of those winter months. So I decided to supplement our budget by driving a taxi cab for a local firm within Folkestone. At first it was only part time, with maybe two to three evenings a week. It wasn't long though before I was working full time. It was the only way in which you could make a living out of it. The hours were getting longer and longer and I was seeing less and less of Anja and the children and when I did manage to get time off, it was spent sleeping. But the money helped out during the winter months and kept me from signing on the dole again. However, it was never the amount that I had made on the construction site. Even with Anja now working part time and earning good money we still found it hard going. Financial demands were coming in from all sides and we could not pay half of them. We were facing financial ruin within less than a year of purchasing our new home.

The pressure grew and there was a great risk involved now. Not only could we lose the house and everything within, but also each other. The pressure of not being able to keep our financial agreements was having a more serious affect than we bargained for ... now our relationship together was on the very brink of being terminated. Tempers were frayed and often erupted into verbal abuse that exploded into sometimes physical contact and confrontation.

When our anger had subsided somewhat, we sat down and had a rethink about the whole situation that was confronting us. If we wanted to stay together as a family, then we would have to move carefully and quickly to solve our immediate crisis. The plan was simple enough. I took a couple of weeks off from taxi driving and only worked a couple of nights a week. The rest of the time I spent on converting the house into separate rooms (five in all). We could let the rooms to the construction workers who by now were coming into Folkestone to begin work on the Channel Tunnel. We could quite easily ask £100 a week per room. That was £500 a week ... enough to pay the mortgage and all of our debt we had accumulated over the months, as well as having £1,000 a month over to put into a bank somewhere. It was a brilliant idea.

In the meantime we would go and live in Holland, where it seems the work was plentiful and the money extremely good. Not only that, but no one knew of my past, so it would be like starting again.

We were trying to organise everything ourselves so the plan would run smoothly before departure but each time we would run into another snag along the way. The bailiffs were now beginning to knock on the door demanding money. And before long we had to involve a solicitor to try and tidy up some of the financial mess we had gotten ourselves into.

The house was all ready and partly furnished to receive the lets. Unfortunately we chose to put everything into the solicitor's hands for him to manage everything for a modest fee.

Anja and the children had by this time left for Holland and was arranging private accommodation for us to move into. It all seemed a spur of the moment decision but we were faced with some daunting alternatives otherwise. And it felt at the time that this was the best solution of all, for us to risk.

I was fortunate to have married a Dutch woman: as all the processes of obtaining the necessary documentation allowing me to reside and work within the Netherlands were quite simple. Otherwise things may have been difficult (the Dutch are notoriously renowned for their bureaucracy).

This was my first real taste of the Dutch way of life. I had only made brief visits prior to moving out of England and most of those were spent visiting Anja's family.

The culture is very similar to our own in fact and shares with the British close historic connections that intertwine. But that's about all I'm afraid. My first encounters with them as a whole was of being a friendly almost gentle people. My views differ now of course, now that I can converse with them in their own language. But I guess each country has its own faults and if allowed, I too, can become severe in criticising most things.

Work was forthcoming and, as promised, plentiful. I worked as a painter and decorator for a while but, oddly, found it difficult to be working for someone else. I had been rather spoilt back in England where I had been almost my own boss and left to my own decision-making of how things ought to be done. But here I felt as though I was always being watched and my work commented on (again, the Dutch have their own method of doing things and woe to you if you should do them differently). But, what the heck, I was a true Brit, stubborn as they themselves were and carried on doing the things my way. I guess they took it too much the hard way and they really began to make things kind of hard from then on. I stuck with it though for as long as I possibly could under the circumstances. In the end, my temper got the better of me and I lost control towards one of the charge hands. He had always had a problem with me, from the very beginning.

On this occasion he started to throw his temper at me by throwing objects towards and at me. That was it. I picked up an air compressor and threw it sideways towards him, only to find he was quick off the mark and somehow dodged out of the way. Having seen it was going to miss him, I picked up one of the air lines that was being dragged along the floor from the compressor and attacked him violently by pinning him up against a wall and shoving the hose in his mouth, threatening to fill his internal parts with toxic paint should he ever start again. The shock took us both by surprise. It all happened within a split second. After that, he refused to work on the same job as me and I was moved to another site, but decided to leave shortly afterwards on a mutual understanding.

I found it awkward to say the least, when I had to explain to my wife that I was no longer in employment. But as always, she learned to forgive me quickly, helped pick me up from the scrap heap and pushed me forward.

For a while I worked with various employers through an employment agency – anything from working on a building site and erecting scaffolding to working in a steel mill – anything would do.

Bad news from England was soon to follow. Our intended plan of letting our home was aborted. Things didn't seem to go as well as expected and so we decided just to go ahead and sell the house rather than return and face a barrage of unpaid bills and explanations to people.

Anja was also pregnant and I couldn't bear the thought of having to bring her back to England to face all this unwanted pressure. So we cut our losses in the UK. And, with a rather reduced profit from the sale of the house, brought a holiday cottage in the Belgian countryside. At least we could get away most weekends for a break.

Another surprise – a good one this time – happened when a few of my mates arrived on our doorstep one weekend. They had been working as welders and steel erectors for an agency in Holland for the past three months. Somehow they had managed to get hold of my address from friends back in Wellingborough and decided to pay us a visit.

While I had tried to avoid friendship with some of them (owing to their involvement with the criminal fraternity and with drugs), it was great to see them all again after so long a time had passed. I suddenly realised how much I had in fact missed the social contact with my own countrymen. I began to realise too, my own faults and how I felt towards their friendship. I began to compare my loyalty to them with theirs to me. I'm afraid my loyalty towards them came way down the list. For here they all were, offering me some sort of comfort in their friendship towards me, accepting me for what I was and without any mention of conditions. I was made to feel very humble among them all and really thanked God that I still had some friends left.

During the course of the weekend, we got to talk about work and I mentioned that I was not particularly happy the way things were turning out for me. Without any hesitation from any of them, I was told to come and work with them as steel erectors. At first I thought that they were joking with me, but no, they were quite serious. And within a few days I was working all over Holland with them. This meant that I was working away from home all week and some weekends but the money was great and it was all tax free. It solved many problems at the time. But much more it was a time of being around other Brits and sharing some deep thoughts between us.

I guess it was also a time of great change for me, feeling somewhat more secure in a foreign country and yet among my own kind. I began to endeavour to search out many wrong things within my life and tried to become more spiritual minded.

Bad news came from England. My father had been taken into hospital. Fear gripped me, as I heard that he was now dying. My father and I never got on as father and son should, especially when I was trying to grow up. At times I hated him and shared with the rest of my family in blaming him for all the wrong he ever did the family. It was only towards the end of his life that I began to rediscover my father and some of his ways. I also discovered more of myself during this time and realised how very wrong I had been towards him in the past. I share with my father some of his greatest weaknesses upon this earth and realise only some of the torment he must have gone through in this life. My agony now is that I hope he forgives me for my ignorance of him and his love of me. My understanding of my father came much too late in my life, perhaps it would have made all the difference if he had been granted longer upon this earth and I would have had the time to get to know him better ... who knows?

Before me and my wife was a dying man. I closed the door quietly so as not to disturb his fragile sleep and thoughts. The stench of the hospital brought with it past memories of my mother's death and all the anguish that was sure to follow his departure. I wanted so much to hold him in my arms that day, for ever. But somehow I just couldn't do it.

It was some days later on our return from the UK that we received the news that he had passed away. An empty feeling came over me as I reflected upon my memories of him and of his loneliness in this life and even unto his death. At least I held his hand and told him that I loved him before he left.

I couldn't explain the feelings I had when Anja finally gave birth to my son (Mitchell Bourne-Kendall Gregory). The even greater wonder of why I had been so richly blessed gave room to even a deeper search within of what life was all about. I promised him that he would never want for the things in this world that I had found it impossible to achieve.

Within six months: all work on the construction trade came to a halt for us and we were suddenly faced with another desire ... to return to England or stay in Holland. While the work was more available here I was desperate to be around my own countrymen. The choice, therefore, wasn't as difficult as I

126

thought. We had some money in the bank and thought that perhaps at least it would be enough to start up a small business of sorts. I was determined whatever we chose to do in the end I would not rely on the system in England on our return.

I left Holland a week or so before Anja and the kids. I had to see where we would try to make a living and get a feeling for the place ... as of yet we were still unsure of where we would go.

After a few days in England I somehow ended up in the wonderful city of Sheffield, south Yorkshire. It was really the first time I had lived in a large city since my vagrant days of living on the streets of London, but this time was a little different. I had some money in my pocket.

I had a look at a few private places to rent just on the outskirts of Sheffield, but found them a bit expensive and a little too isolated. By chance I was walking within the city centre of Sheffield and came across an estate agent and, as luck would have it, found an ideal place to rent – A Victorian house situated in the nicer part of the city and partially furnished. Anja and the kids would love it. I paid the deposit and a month in advance for the keys and then quickly telephoned home to tell them the news.

I left shortly afterwards on the next available flight back to Holland quite excited of the thought that we were coming home to England. I spent most of the time pondering on what I should do about the work situation, thinking it best that I should keep within my highly acquired knowledge of painting/decorating and scaffolding: I decided there and then that I would try to start up my own business within that sphere of things.

The plane landed at Rotterdam airport and Anja was there to meet me. A large smile upon her face greeted me and a welcome hug was all that I needed to confirm that we were doing the right thing in moving back to England.

Within that same month we had moved into our new home and I was up and running my own business. Things seemed to go smoothly and new business was not difficult to find. It felt good to be my own boss at last. For just this once it felt that I had conquered life and felt proud of it. And it was just for once that I felt this feeling of a little success and happiness in my life.

> The greatest Miracle in life ... is not to turn water into
>   wine!
> Or even to be able to walk upon the waters!
> The greatest Miracle of all ... is simply to walk upon
>   this earth.

Life has a terrible habit of biting back, especially when we think everything is going so damn well. Why should it be different for me? Again, we were looking at the possibilities of purchasing our own home. Things were doing well, although I hit a slump in work ... but no doubt it would pick up again when the weather got better.

We decided to look further north of the country for somewhere suitable and away from the inner city of Sheffield, not because we disliked Sheffield, but because we found the pace of life too fast for us. We looked everywhere while our mortgage proposal was being confirmed and approved by one of the building societies.

We found a nice place in Co. Durham. Darlington to be precise ... and going quite cheap in comparison with the same sort of houses offered further south. We envisaged no problems in getting a loan ... but how wrong we were to be. I could not give the lenders acceptable accounts for the past three years and we were declined. It was devastating to both of us. We tried every possible way in getting around the refusal ... but with no success.

Instead, we came across an extremely large farmhouse with lots of land with it, for a long leasehold tenancy on one of the royal estates in Co. Durham. It compensated for the loan refusal. It was absolutely wonderful, and set in among the high rugged landscape of that area. We both fell in love with it and thought of it as a blessing. We didn't stop to think of the many things we should have thought of beforehand. Nothing was further from us other than we had to have this house.

So it was that we moved into it more or less straight away. It was fantastic and the children loved to be amongst the wildlife and around nature. We too would spend most of our free time together exploring many things of this vast wilderness where we now lived. It was no longer a working farm, although we did keep a few chickens and a couple of dogs (the size of horses). We soon made new friends with our nearest neighbours (half a mile away) and felt we were accepted straight away into the farming community.

Most of my work was being done in the south of England by now, so I was spending most of my time away from home yet again. It seemed that wherever we moved, work was in the opposite direction. I guess really it was my mistake as I should have done rather more market research than I ever did before embarking on this dramatic move.

It was also a time of bad economics ... not only for me, but for the whole country. The building trade as a whole was going through a particularly bad patch and the recovery rate was not looking good for entrepreneurs such as me. Everyone connected to the building trade was finding it rough and trade ceasing was commonplace throughout. Again, the winter months seemed to destroy us financially, through my own stupidity mostly in not taking too great a care in my outgoings.

The winter here started in early November and lasted until the following April. By that time I too was no longer trading as a painter/decorator. Instead I was trying to learn another trade, at least to fall back on when things were like this. Driving seemed to be the answer: you could always get work as a truck or bus driver. And so I spent a lot of money in getting all the necessary licences and diplomas to obtain something that I could do when times were rough.

For a while I managed to get work as a bus driver with a local company, although the wages were not good. At least it was a job. And it gave me some good experience in driving. It was not to last long though. Somehow they stumbled upon my forgotten criminal record and, when I took it upon myself to do someone a charitable deed without notice to themselves, I was instantly dismissed. I tried to appeal against the decision, but no such luck. My past criminal record was always before me. It seemed whenever I worked for an employer in England, I was to be confronted with my past.

I worked for another employer as a national truck driver and decided not to be to honest about my past. Invented past employment references so it became more difficult for anyone to trace me down. It had to be done though. And I felt justified in doing it. My family depended on me being able to support them. It helped to keep things almost legal within my plight to gain employment when I decided to change my name by deed poll (the best thing I ever did). I was given a new identity. It was almost like being born again with a new lease of life. No one could now produce any of my past records. I felt I had literally earned the right to be able to start life anew.

I stayed with my employer for a few months and gained ever-increasing knowledge of being a truck driver and then, when I thought the time was right, I changed from being a national driver to an international driver (it was better money).

We tried for so long to hold on to the farm we had so much loved, but with ever-increasing debts to be paid off from my business going bankrupt, it was a losing battle and we were given notice to quit.

It was devastating for the whole of the family. And from a mansion-type house we moved into something resembling an outhouse. It had its own charm, I guess, but it was totally inadequate and in urgent need of repair. And very, very cold when the weather took a turn for the worse.

The work was frequent with many trips abroad and I quite enjoyed my independence as well as the solitude. Driving a truck weighing over 38 tons is not as easy as it appears to most people and is one of the most stressful jobs I've ever done. It's hard work, especially when you have deadlines to meet and sleep often becomes a luxury. But it is addictive and is a way of life.

Again we were thinking of how to get over our crisis. Money has always been an incentive in the way we decide things. After all, there isn't a lot you can do in this world without it. And my policy in life is that you have to be prepared to travel wherever you can find the best possible deal in finding work. And this I've always done.

Holland again became our focus point. I knew that an international truck driver could always get a job in Holland. The wages were a lot higher in comparison with the UK.

Whereas a trucker could earn £250/300 a week by UK standards, a trucker working for a Dutch company could earn in excess of £800/1,000 a week ... and that's how I decided to move the family again. Of course, there was more to it than just that.

I've never forgiven England and the system it employs at never letting people forget the hideous mistakes they have made in the past. And yet I love it so dearly. But I could never return to inhabit her shores again for these reasons.

I've worked as an international truck driver in Holland for the past seven years now and, at long last, I've managed to get my act together financially. The quality of family life has improved tremendously as time went by and my restless feet grew accustomed to a new-found security in regular work.

Tragedy struck two years ago ... with another crisis within the family that had to be resolved. I was unloading my truck, when the side frame to the trailer collapsed and sent me hurtling backwards towards the ground some 16 feet below. Remembering how to control a rearward fall from those army days, I prevented myself from being paralysed or suffering an even worse fate. However, I injured my neck and broke both my arms in four places. One of my arms now has an assortment of metal plates within and will be a permanent disability to me, preventing me from driving any large vehicle or doing any amount of physical work.

For these past two and a half years, I've been troubled about the future and how will I survive in supporting my family. But the more I reflect upon my life and analyse the situation that resulted from my accident, the more I'm convinced of a greater force at work within my life. I know, you have heard it all before.

132

For the first time in my life, I've been made (by one circumstance or another) physically and mentally to lie down and take time out for myself, to reflect on all of my life and to try to piece together some of the events that have taken their toll on my character.

It hasn't been easy and the writing of this book has had a greater impact upon my life than has life itself. It was designed only to help me pass some of the time away while I recovered from my injuries. And that was all of its intention. But it was while I was learning to write and to put some of my thoughts on paper during its construction, that I found much more of myself and, in so doing, found so much more of the God I was searching for within my life.

A lot of tear shedding was done while I reflected on my life and some of the tragic circumstances that happened when I was still in adolescence and I found little time for comfort from anyone or anything (for I was completely alone). Maybe you can't understand some of the tragedy I went through because of my simple use of the English language in explaining my feelings (I'm working on it). But for some, I hope at least, that it has its profoundness in its writing. I'm a simple man ... and the only complicated part of me was my life and how I chose to live it. Not all my decisions were the right ones but whether right or wrong in the making, they have helped in the shaping of my changing character today. And perhaps if I had not made so many tragic mistakes along the way, my life would be naked and incomplete. For now I'm a little wiser. And can feel so much more of the compassion for others in their tormented lives.

Throughout my life, my endless wonder and question became: what was man's purpose in life? Indeed, what was my own purpose? What was I living for? An answer never seemed to come, especially when often I found myself encased within the turmoils of a prison. I was fortunate in having a strong will to get me through some of the times in my life.

More often than not and unfortunately in most circumstances within my life, it was my own will that failed and deceived me. It took me the best part of my life to realise that in life, there is another will, a greater will than our own, a divine will.

I guess that all men have a strong will but it fails them like it failed me and undoubtedly will fail you some day. My will today is simply drawn from strength – an almighty strength and belief in God. It has become an endless hunger. And nothing seems to fill the gap or satisfy my appetite other than knowing more of myself and that of God.

I mentioned 'a new wind that has filled my sails'. I'm not a religious freak ... or anything like that. A belief in an effortless adoration may be a religion for an angel but never for me.

Mine is the uncovering of the face ... my face, that will one day look upon God's. It is about knowing myself and trying to perfect myself constantly. The extraordinary thing is that there is no special formula or recipe for this endeavour from within. It's a lone path to walk and it would never be the same for others as it has been for me. The final outcome would always be different ... it is important therefore that I say little else.

But remember it was with some mixed feelings as well as trepidation that I have compiled these miscellaneous pieces of thoughts and events that have occurred within my life and have shared only some of the association with God with you. It's up to you. And only if you wish to seek him further.

To many, these thoughts will not represent a consistent or

indeed a coherent representation or statement towards my past life, let alone any mention of a particular denominational faith that I now have. And I'm fully aware that often in my expression of my feelings that they may appear to be sometimes repetitive as well as imprecise and often contradictory. For this I ask forgiveness! This was about some of my life and about the changing of my character (not yet perfected). Altered in direction over the many years by slight degrees and not by some blinding light upon a Damascus Road somewhere.

Writing this book was the beginning of an inner search: not yet written ... of hidden discoveries within my own soul and not always a better part but often a deeper darker and more sinister part.

The message ... is not to conform too rigorously to the world or societies: but to allow ourselves to be transformed by truth within.

This is now my future. This is now my goal. My place upon this earth.

Part Two

Deliverance

Preface

With some diffidence I have compiled these thoughts: in all, associated in some way or another with my attitude and feelings about the Christian faith and a greater search from within.

My pitiful life is changing dramatically and has over these recent years altered in its direction. In fact, nothing could be further from the truth. For me, life from a very early age has been an assault course of a great many hazards and stumbling blocks; and will be I'm sure until my very end.

A series of consequences and many wrong decisions and turnings, with false destinations, has now led me to an even greater discovery . . . that of being myself. That singular fleshy humanoid that holds so many secrets within: the darker and lighter parts that each of us possess within one body.

Each new day I'm discovering something new within: not always a better part but often a darker, more sinister side of my life. An awesome awareness that from this one body

139

comes the capabilities of committing good and evil. And the more I search, then always the more I can find within what I'm lacking. But what of this, you may ask yourselves.

It is from this inner search that I've learnt that when each of us falls from the grace of God, or we are guilty of committing some hideous crime or wrongdoing that would undoubtedly trouble our inner peace, then we pick ourselves up without the inclination to linger but to carry on regardless, with the notion that one day, however indistinct, we will all reach a destination.

The message is not to rigorously conform to the world or societies: but to allow ourselves to be transformed by truth from within. We are all subjected to transforming influences; in that we do not literally transform ourselves, it is something outside the thermometer that produces a change from within and likewise I feel it is something outside the soul of man that will produce the inner moral change.

But the change we may desire within and have strived towards cannot be produced or reproduced. It is literally wrought upon us by those moulding hands beyond our own. I have many defects: one in particular bothers me to the extent that on occasion I've felt like suicide and have been too embarrassed to confide in anyone other than God. I have been brought to my wit's end as well as to my knees, without any reprieve or cure. My radical methods of sanctification and forgiveness were and sometimes still are, I feel, an attempt to generate from within that which can only be generated and literally wrought upon from without.

In science according to the first law of motion, everybody continues in his first state of rest or in a uniform motion in a straight line; except in so far as he may be compelled by such impressed forces to change that first state. This may also be the first law also of man's faith in God and of himself in Christianity. Every person's character remains as it is; or continues in the direction in which it is going, until it feels compelled by impressed forces or events to change that state.

My failure therefore, as with so many in similar situations, has been a failure to expose myself these impressed forces. There is the clay: as there is the potter. I only tried to succeed in getting the clay to mould the clay. But in itself it is not all. If all these reflected and varied thoughts from my life are common and patent to us all, then how close the writing and how complete the record within the soul?

Are we only mere mirrors of design of some grander reflector? And do we each reflect the fleeting things we see? Or transfer them into our own innermost substance and hold dear in permanent preservation the things that they reflect. No one knows how the soul can hold these things. No process in chemistry or science, not even by phenomenon within our nature or even a chapter or two in necromancy can even begin to help us in this understanding of our deeper soul search and this amazing operation of change. No one other than God knows how the miracle is done.

All things that I've seen, known, felt and believed of the surrounding world are now with me and have become part of me: and in part, are me. I am therefore changed into their image. Though they do not adhere to me, they are in many ways transfused through me in character. I cannot erase or alter them in any way for they are not necessary within my memory, they are in me. My soul is as they have filled it, made it and have left it.

These events that have taken place within my life are the makers of my character and of whom I am today. And within their hand (God) are the beauty and deformities of this world, together with life and death. When the soul is presented with anything of these no power on earth can hinder two things happening ... it must be absorbed into the very depths of our souls and for ever reflected back again from our character.

We are what we are by the impacts of those who have surrounded us: for those who surround themselves with the highest will undoubtedly be those who will change into the highest. And likewise, if we surround ourselves with the lowest, then we run a greater risk of becoming low ourselves.

There are some people in whose company we are constantly at our best. And when in their company we cannot think mean thoughts or speak ungenerously of them. Their sheer presence is elevation and brings with it sanctity and almost purification towards the soul. Here even on the common plain of life, talking our language and working side by side and walking the same roads, are sanctifiers of souls; here breathing earthly clay is heaven. Here our energies become charged even through a temporal medium with a virtue of regeneration. If to live with others, diluted to the millionth degree with this virtue of the highest, can exalt and purify our natures ... then what bounds can be set to the influence of Christ?

To have lived with or even associated with Socrates must have made one wise. With Aristides, just. Francis of Assisi must have made one gentle. Savonarola: strong. The list goes on. But to have lived with Christ must have made one like Christ: a Christian.

Throughout the day our actions, down to the last detail, will do homage to that early vision. Yesterday I thought mostly of myself. Today the poor and the needy may come across my path and I will feed them. The tempted and the afflicted, the saddened and the helpless will gather about, and each will I befriend.

Where were they all yesterday? Where they were today, but I failed to see them. It is with reflected light that the poor and the afflicted are seen. The things which were not previously seen are visible. And for these short few hours we live, this eternal life, the eternal life of our faith, is simply the life of a higher vision of our faith and becomes an attitude, a mirrored reflector set at the right angle.

In reflection on my past and that of my experiences, the part that stands out which I remember the most vividly is that which has had some conscious association with God. The rest is pale and thin and has been worn away by time itself, and lies like the clouds on the horizon. Systems, doctrines, measured methods and what may be interpreted as the necessities of a mechanical or indeed somewhat of an external part of worship (in the part in which our senses would recognise): all this seems to have withered and has fallen off like dried leaves in the autumn sun. But the part that has taken hold of God: that part still abides deep within.

1

Amending the Ways We Once Walked

We may all be ashamed of the many wrong thoughts and vices that have lain deep within our lives and that have somehow led us to our present situation. Nothing other than guilt has finally presented itself, face to face, with our very soul and the life we are leading. We may all desire to lead a more spiritual life and walk upon another road but as yet have failed to discover it.

'And as our eyes observe others: so then, are we ourselves observed.' Oh! how comfortable and sweet it is to see others devout and fervent, regular and seemingly well disciplined in their chosen profession and belief. But are you like me, feeling so sad in walking a disorderly life and practising very little if not nothing of what we are called to do.

How painful it has become to neglect our own vocations, concerning ourselves with things that do not concern us, our very purpose in life seems all to have vanished. Through gross negligence, we have become lukewarm and somewhat

144

disillusioned with leading a spiritual life. We have found only trouble upon trouble and on each of these sides we only seem to be suffering anguish and turmoil. And why? Perhaps because we no longer have that hidden inner comfort within and are hindered from seeking any from being without.

Almost with great ease our lives seem to be looking for laxity in direction and now we are always experiencing some sort of dire straits within, our lives and everything within becoming displeasing to the very core of our soul. What can be more at rest than a single eye? And who can be more free than one who desires nothing upon this earth?

Nothing has become more troublesome or even a worse adversary to our soul than ourselves when not agreeing well with the spirit. Most of us, therefore, have walked the paths of unrighteousness and are fully aware of the sins we have committed: and as to the roads we shall endeavour to walk upon in future, we can only ask for guidance from a more worthy spirit, together with forgiveness, for life itself is nothing more than the temptation of the flesh.

In all truth, lofty words make nothing of a man becoming just or in anyway holy or spiritually inclined, and you must forgive me if sometimes my writing makes you feel otherwise, but the possibility of living a virtuous life may at least make us dear to God. Therefore our own deep compunction and the way we sometimes feel is in all probability better than if we were to realise its true definition.

The doctrine of Christ surpasseth all the doctrines and whosoever has the spirit within will I'm sure find within its study a hidden manna.

It happens that many hearing the gospel frequently are little affected by its profound message to us as individuals.

This is probably because we have not yet always found that right spirit of God that is within all of us somewhere.

If only we could withdraw our minds and hearts from the love and lusts of visible things and turn ourselves to things that are invisible. For we all tend to follow the flesh and visible things that only succeed in the defilement of our conscience and losing the grace of God. Our continuing to follow such things that are, after all, punished grievously by our own conscience can only be futile and is in itself, vanity.

Our eyes are not content or satisfied with seeing. Or our ears with only hearing. It is important, therefore, that we must begin to study the withdrawal from the love of desire and the want of things visible.

They that know themselves well are mean in their own eyes: and are not always delighted with the praises of others. For if we knew everything that there is to know in this world and were not in a state of charity, how would it help us in the sight of God, who would judge us by our deeds?

An excessive desire of knowledge is sometimes better left alone because there is found within much distraction and deceit. And those who are of much learning are quite happy to be called wise. But there are many things the knowledge of which is of little or no profit to the soul or indeed the life we now seek. It is probably therefore unwise to attend to things other than what may serve towards our salvation.

Words cannot always satisfy the soul, but maybe a good life gives ease to our minds and a pure conscience should afford us with a greater confidence in God. The more and better we strive to become then the more heavy will be our judgement, until our lives become more accustomed to spiritual living. Our own knowledge, which has been given in accordance, that we each may know many things and to be able to understand well enough, is in itself a realisation that at the same time there is much more we are ignorant of. Trying not to be high minded in all these and to realise one's ignorance is a sign of humility.

> If we would but learn:
> Anything to the purpose
> Love to be unknown.
> And esteemed as nothing.
> *Imitation of Christ*, Thomas à Kempis

Perfection of oneself is not to esteem oneself better. Can you tell how long you will remain in a good state? We are all frail but think no one more frail than yourself.

Our opinions and our senses often deceive us and perceive but very little. What does it profit us to engage ourselves in an empty discussion, about obtuse and obscure matters? For the ignorance of which we shall surely not be questioned at the end of the day.

Truth, I feel, will teach by itself not by words or by figures that all too quickly pass away. But as it is, in itself.

It is great folly to neglect our daily needs that are all too necessary for our spiritual growth. Instead we busy ourselves with things curious and hurtful towards the soul. What need do we concern ourselves about questions of great philosophy? For, when the time is right, the Eternal Word shall speak to our inner soul and set us all free from many opinions and lifestyles.

I believe one word is all things and from one, all things speak. And this is the very beginning. Without this one word, no one can understand or judge rightly.

O, Truth my God, make me one with you in everlasting Love and fellowship. As we strive towards perfection in this life, it is with attendance of some degree of imperfection from within, that all our speculations have certain obscurities. Surely, therefore, a more humble knowledge of ourselves is a surer way to God than any deeper search after science that offers nothing in comforting our souls. Learning is not to be blamed, nor the mere knowledge of anything which is good in itself and ordained by God but a good conscience and virtuous living should always be preferred before it.

If only we would use as much diligence in rooting out our evil vices and planting virtues as we do in proposing question upon question, there would not be such great evils committed, nor scandals amongst us. But we are indeed flesh and of this earth, and in our journey along the roads of life tend only to commit many wrongs and atrocities.

Perhaps we are all lost somewhere in that imagination of how we should conduct ourselves and live our own life. And perhaps too it is because we all desire and choose to become great in some special way, to be accepted as a somebody in this demanding world and get noticed. Perhaps this is where a great evil lies within us all: striving to become something that we are not destined to become. And never being able to reach our intended direction makes only for further mistakes along the way.

While I believe that we all possess the spirit of God within, I also believe that we should humble ourselves in wisdom and realise that we do not always have equal access to this spirit, otherwise we would all be singing the same tune and have equal thoughts of the doctrines of this world. All of us hold much within and yet we all learn from one another.

148

So as the four great seasons upon this earth!
Each must wait for the appointed time...
Each of them different...
Executing its own task of commitment.

Our weakness is that we are all too often ready to speak and believe something of which is evil than that which is good. But if you know man's weakness and are aware of yours and realise that we too are prone to evil and very subject to fail in both words and in thought, then maybe it is for the better that we must not be to rash in our actions of judgement upon others, nor to maintain obstinately our own opinions.

Don't believe every man's word, nor presently tell others the thing we have heard or believe: it would be wise and better to take counsel from a conscientious man or woman and to take instruction from one that is better, than to follow your own devices. I believe that truth therefore should only be sought after in Holy Scriptures, and not in eloquences.

Try to read the Scriptures with that self-same spirit in which they were written and search for profit in them rather than subtlety of speech. Remember too that we should read willingly both devout as well as simple books, as those are high and profound. Do not let the authority of the writer offend you, whether he was of little or of great learning, but let the love of pure truth lead you to read.

Inquire not who has said this but attend to what is said. God speaks to us in many ways without respect of persons. We must not let curiosity hinder us in reading the Scriptures when we attempt to understand in our own small way and discuss that which should be simply passed over. If you want to receive profit, then read with simplicity, humility and that of your own faith. Willingly consult and hear with silence the words that you hear, and refrain from the displeasures of the parables of our elders; for they too have not been spoken without their cause.

We must all learn within ourselves to overcome temptations. The person that is not perfectly dead to himself is soon tempted and overcome with trifling things. He, as with us all, is weak in spirit and carnal and inclined to less sensible things; he can therefore hardly withdraw himself wholly from earthly desires.

Are we not all saddened when we withdraw unto ourselves? And when we withdraw from our worldly desires, are we not all easily moved to anger if any resist us? To pursue with our inclinations is to be presently tormented with guilt and torment of our conscience because we have followed our own passions and they help little in seeking the peace in which we are seeking.

This is why there is very little peace. And only by sheer force of resistance of our passions, and not in serving them, can we find true peace of the heart. There is then no peace in the heart of carnal persons: nor with the addicted who look to outward and worldly things. But only in the fervent and spiritual. This is why whenever we desire anything inordinately we are quickly disquieted with ourselves.

We must try also to refrain from the glory of riches if we have them, but glory in God, who gives all things but mostly desires to give himself above all things.

Don't boast of your stature or of your physique, or the beauty of your bodies, which after all, are to often spoiled and disfigured by sickness.

If we have any good, then believe better things in others, so that at least we may preserve humility within ourselves.

It will do us no harm to esteem ourselves the least of all
But great harm to prefer ourself to another.

2

Subjection and Obedience

To live under a superior and in obedience is a great thing and not to be at our own disposal is much more secure than to be in authority.

But many of us are subjected to obedience more out of a necessity than for the love of God. Such as these suffer and easily repine and gain little freedom of their own mind unless they submit themselves with all of their whole heart for God's sake.

We have all run away from God but did we ever find peace? Did we ever find rest? Our own imagination and the changing of places has made us all restless and to some extent deceived us all. Promises of fame, fortune – they are not the solutions they've promised to be.

Everyone is guilty of being desirous and of acting according to their own liking. And are more inclined to such as of our own mind. But if God be amongst us then we must sometimes give up our own opinions for the sake of peace.

Are we so wise as to be able to know all things fully?
Trust not, too much of our own mind,
But be willing also to hear the mind of others.
Our own opinion, although be it good
Yet for God's sake we leave it: to follow that of another
May become more profitable to ourselves.

We, as only humans, are quickly defiled and ensnared with
vanity and evil thoughts: better then to flee the tumult and
the teaching of men as much as we can. For the treating of
worldly affairs only hinders us from the real truth, although
they be discoursed with such simple intentions.

Sometimes I have wished that I had been silent and that I
had not been in the company of others. But why is it we are so
willing to talk with others and discourse with one another,
since we seldom return to silence without feeling hurt towards
our own conscience for having said too much. The reason I
guess is, by talking with others, we seek some sort of comfort
from one another, and it gladly eases the heart. But wearied by
various thoughts, we are all very willing to talk and share with
others what we have most loved and desired within our past
lives or even that which is to the contrary to us. Remember
the old days!

Alas, it is often in vain and to no fruitful purpose to
reminisce on our past. This so easily becomes a bad custom
and we begin to neglect our spiritual advancement and so do
much towards recklessness of thought and of speech. Only
devout conferences concerning spiritual things help much
towards spiritual progress: especially where persons of the
same mind are associated together in God.

We are too much taken up with fancy thoughts of our own
passions and those of others and are too solicitous about

transitory things: seldom do we perfectly overcome so much as one vice within ourselves; nor can this be attributed to earnestly searching towards our progress, therefore we remain cold and tepid.

If only we were perfectly clean of impure thought and no way entangled interiorly, then we might be able to relish things more and experience something of a more heavenly contemplation. If only we were free from all passions and lusts! And whenever we would meet with any small or great adversity we were not too quickly dejected so as to turn towards human consolation. If only we would endeavour to strive as a valiant people, to stand in the battle, then doubtless we would see the Lord helping us.

If we therefore place our progress in religion but in outward observances only, our devotion will all too quickly be at an end. Put the axe to the roof, that being purged from these passions we may at least possess a quiet mind.

We would think by now that our eagerness and continual improvement would in fact be greater each day. But now the feeling is esteemed a greater matter if at least we can retain some of that self-same zeal we first encountered within our search. Make no doubt about it. Searching from within is very hard. And then to attempt living by what we find is even harder.

It is hard to break from our old customs and even harder it seems to go against our own free will. But if we cannot overcome these small things, then how can we ever achieve or overcome the more difficult?

It is best we try therefore to resist the first inclinations of temptation in the beginning and try to break off from our evil habits, otherwise, take it from me, we will only increase our difficulties in overcoming them.

154

There is an advantage to all adversity in each of our lives and if nothing else it allows us to enter into ourselves so that we may know that at the very least we are in a state of banishment and therefore not to place our hopes in anything of this world. It also remains good that to some degree we will all suffer contradictions and others will always have an imperfect opinion of us: even when our intentions seem well in thought. For these things often help us to find within ourselves some kind of humility, defending us, I guess, from vain glory. And within these times we ought to seek God, who is our inward witness, when outwardly we are despised by others and little credit is given us.

When we are troubled or tempted and afflicted with evil thoughts, then it is better we understand what real need we have in God, without whom we can never do good. Always after temptation we are left feeling sorry, and begin to sigh and pray by our own reason of miseries that then we must suffer: we begin to feel low in spirit and wish we could all but once be dissolved and live no more in this painful world. In this moment, and only then, do we perceive that perfection and security cannot exist in this world.

Face it, at this point in our lives, as long as we live in this world, we cannot be without trials and tribulation. Temptation is a part of everyone's life, it is even mentioned in the Scriptures.

Man's life upon earth is a temptation. We ought therefore to be solicitous about our temptations and to watch and pray. None of us is perfect or so holy as not to have imperfect and impure thoughts: sometimes experiencing great temptations within our lives ... and the truth is that we cannot be totally without them. We know that they are troublesome and are grievous to both our bodies and spirit. But remember, they can

155

be very profitable to us; for in them we can become humbled, purified and instructed.

It may be that we are often troubled and tempted by the same temptation many times and in danger then of becoming a person of bad character and falling away from our beliefs and spiritual needs.

We all fail daily because we have within us all the source of temptation, having been born from concupiscence, and when one temptation or tribulation is over another will surely follow. We will always have something to suffer and endure because we have all lost the gift of our original happiness in life.

Many will seek to flee temptation only to fall more grievously into its hold. We cannot overcome by running away. But by patience we shall with God's grace overcome them, rather than by the harshness of our own importunity.

One of my greatest faults is not to possess an altogether consistent mind in my beliefs. And I have found that inconstancy of mind and having at times small confidence in God is the beginning of most of my temptation and tribulation.

We are all too often aware of what we can do but remember: temptation reminds us all and discovers what and who we really are:

> Fire tries iron
> And temptation will try a just man.

It is important that we are watchful, especially in the beginning of our temptation. They say that it is much more easy to resist temptation when it has not suffered to come in at the door of the soul, but has been kept out and resisted at the first knock. Withstand the beginnings: after remedies come much too late. First comes the bare thought to mind, then a strong imagination, afterwards the delight and the evil motion, and then the consent. And thus, little by little, the wickedness gets full entrance when not resisted at the outset.

The longer we are negligent in resisting, then the weaker we become within ourselves and the stronger becomes our enemy. Of course, there are those who will suffer great temptations at the very beginning of our search from within, with others towards the end. But be sure – we will be tempted.

Then there are those who are badly troubled most, if not all, of their lives. Some are but lightly tempted, according to that wisdom and equity of the ordinance of God, who weighs the state and merit of us all and has pre-ordained all, for the salvation of his elect. It is better, therefore, that we do not experience despair when we are tempted, but pray to God with so much the more fervour, that he may help us all in overcoming tribulation.

3

Rashness of Judgement upon Others

If only God was the object of our desire, we should not so easily be disturbed at the resistance of our opinions.

We too often judge things from the heart, and thus lose the true judgement. We must turn our eyes back towards ourselves and see that we do not judge others too harshly. For in judging others, we are often labouring in vain and often make mistakes, remembering that each of us is easily overcome with sin. We must look at ourselves first.

There are many of us who secretly search ourselves in all that we do but are not always sensible of it; we seem also to continue in good peace when things are said and done according to our will and judgement, but if it fall out to the contrary to our desires, we are soon saddened.

Difference of our thoughts and that of our opinions is the probable source of dissension among friends and neighbours alike, together with even the religious and the seemingly devout people. An old custom, therefore, is relinquished with great difficulty, and no man wonders willingly further than he sees fit. If therefore we rely more upon our own reasoning or industry than the virtue that subjects to God, then we will seldom become an enlightened person, for God will have us perfectly subjected to himself, and to transcend all reason by ardent Love.

Judge with compassion and express charity, for without these the outward work profits nothing and no one. But whatever is done out of compassion and charity be it never so little and contemptible, all becomes fruitful.

For God regards more with how much affection and love a person performs a work than that of how much he does. What a person cannot amend within himself or others, then they must bear with patience, until God ordains otherwise. It is perhaps better to suffer our trials with patience, without which our merits are of little worth. God himself knows how to convert all that is evil into good.

Endeavour to be patient in supporting the defects and infirmities of others, of whatever kind; because we too have many things in which others must bear with. We all too willingly and readily would have others to become perfect, and yet we amend so little if not nothing of our own defects. We would speedily and strictly have others corrected, but are not willing to be corrected ourselves.

The large liberty of others who do wrong displeases the majority of us and yet we would not ourselves be denied anything we ask. We ourselves are willing that others should be bound up by laws and yet we suffer nothing of ourselves in anything to be restrained. This is evident in how seldom we weigh our neighbour in the same balance as ourselves. No person is without their burden or without defect. None sufficient for himself only, and none wise enough for himself.

We must begin to bear one another, comfort and assist, instruct and admonish each other.

> Help me, O Lord my God: in my good resolution
> towards you
> And towards all creatures and towards your service.
> Give me grace now, this day, to perfectly begin:
> For all of what I've done so far ... has been nothing.
> *Imitation of Christ*, Thomas à Kempis

We make many strong resolutions and falling away from them happens in many diverse ways, and at the end of the day they probably all depend on God rather than our own wisdom. And in him we must put our trust, whatever is at hand. For we all may be willing to propose our sincerity and convictions: but I believe only God has the power of disposal and therefore the way of mankind is not in his own hands.

As for our part, we can only express our good faith and intentions and can only do what we can to overcome although being apt to fail in many things, yet we must always resolve on something definitive: particularly against the things that hinder us most.

My experience is to endeavour and never altogether be idle but either to be reading, writing, praying or meditating, or at least exercising some sort of physical labour, for the common good. We all stand in need of one kind in times of temptation and another in times of peace and rest.

4

Silence and the Love of Solitude

We should all search for a proper time to withdraw into ourselves for reflection on the benefits of God and to leave all curiosities alone, reading such matters as we would see fit in moving us to compunction rather than to give us occupation. If only we would withdraw ourselves from superfluous talk and idle visits, along with giving ear to rumours and news, we would find times sufficient and proper to employ ourselves in good meditations.

There are those of us who wish and choose to avoid the company of others as much as we can and live unto God in secret. Seneca once said, 'As often as I have been amongst men, I have returned less a man.'

We too often experience this when we talk to others in greater detail or when we feel we have said more than perhaps we should have. It is altogether easier to be silent and not exceed in many spoken words if our aims are to attaining to things spiritual and internal and must be apart from the crowds, because no man appears securely unless he is happy to be unseen. None of us should securely speak but those who love to hold their peace. None should securely preside over another but those who are willing to be subject. None should command another but those who have learned to obey. And none of us should securely rejoice unless we have within us the testimony of a good conscience.

The security of the wicked arises from pride and presumption and they will end only in deceiving themselves. Often they were better in the judgement of men; having been in greater danger by reason of their too great confidence. In many ways, it is probably better then that we are not altogether free from temptations: after all, we are assaulted by them in many cruel ways, making us totally insecure. But if not, then perhaps we would be lifted up in some kind of pride or even go astray too freely after exterior comforts.

Our earthly desires draw us all away at some stage but when the hours have passed, what good does it bring home but a great weight upon our conscience and dissipation of our heart. When we so joyfully go out and about partaking of our lustful desires, how often do we return home to our sorrowful selves. Remembering a merry evening makes a sad morning. So all our carnal joy may, in the end, bring only remorse.

Stay within yourself and search for God from within for we shall never find a greater place to find him. Give to yourself compunction of heart, and you will find devotion. Compunction will open the way to much good.

Levity of our hearts and the little thoughts we have of
    our defects
We'll feel not the sorrows of our soul
But often vainly laugh, when in all good reason we
    ought to weep.

There is no true liberty, nor good joy in this old world, but for those who separate themselves from all that burdens or defiles the conscience. Hence, it is often more profitable and more secure if we have little comfort in this life, especially according to our fleshly desires.

When we have perfect compunction then, and only then, does this world seem bitter and burdensome.

The subjects for just grief and interior compunction are our own devices of vice and wrongdoings, in which we lie so entangled within that seldom are we able to even contemplate on heavenly things. Often, it is the want of the spirit that makes our wretched body so easily complain.

We must all therefore pray to God that he may give us all a spirit of compunction.

5

Man of Miseries

Why are we troubled because things do not succeed within us according to our will and desire? And who is there that has all things according to his own will?

Neither I, nor you nor any man upon this earth. There is no person upon this earth without some sort of trouble or affliction, be he king or pope. We are miserable whatever we turn towards ... unless it is to God.

The weak and unstable talk of how rich, and of how great or mighty and powerful some appear to be: but if only we would attend ourselves to heavenly things, then we would see that all these temporal things and suggestions are indeed nothing: but unstable and burdensome, because they are never possessed without some sort of anxiety and fear.

Our happiness consists of not having temporal things in abundance but a moderate competency should suffice. The more spiritual minded we are then the more pleasant our lives will become and many things we do will become distasteful to us because we will understand and clearly see the many repugnant defects in human corruption.

We are subject to many necessities of nature, which are themselves of a great misery and affliction, when in all probability we only desire to be released from the majority of them and remain free from all vices. For the inward person is very much burdened with the necessities of the body in this world: and it is so much sorrow and woe to ourselves if we do not know our own misery.

We are for the most part senseless people and infidels at heart, who lie buried deep in earthly things, so as to relish nothing but the desires of our flesh. Wretches of misery, who will at the end find to their own cost how vile was that which they so much loved.

God really has made no account of what pleased the flesh or indeed of what flourished. But Christ, along with his devout believers, had their whole hope and intention to aspire to eternal things. Their whole desire tended upwards, to things everlasting and invisible, fearing that the love of things visible might draw them down to things below.

Why will we put off our resolution from day to day? Stand up! And begin this very moment with God. Now is the time for doing and now is the time to fight. And now is the proper time to amend your life.

Both you and I must not lose our confidence in spiritual things and progressing; there is still that time, our hour has not yet passed.

When we are troubled and afflicted, then this is the time to gain merit. But remember, that as long as we carry this frail body, we cannot be without sin, nor live this life without uneasiness or sorrow.

We would fain be at rest from all our misery but because we

have lost our innocence by sin, this is where we have lost our true happiness. Therefore, we must express our patience and learn to wait for God until iniquity passes away and this mortality has been consumed and swallowed up in life.

> Oh! How frail human and earthly spirits are!
> We seem always prone to vices and failures.
> For today we may have indeed confessed our sin to God
> But tomorrow we may again commit that of what we
>   have already confessed.
>   *Imitation of Christ*, Thomas à Kempis

And then for this reason only, we ought to humble ourselves and never think much of ourselves since we are all frail and inconstant, asking what will become of us in the end? And why should we bother ourselves with searching for inner peace with God, knowing that we shall quickly become lukewarm and fail constantly? But it is of great importance that we begin again and again and not succumb to rest and excepting failures as if we had already achieved and attained some kind of peace and security when there doesn't appear any mark of true sanctity in our lives.

This is why we all need to be trained over and over, again and again, rather like good novices, in all the best rules.

And, as time goes by, and we reflect on our goings and on where we are at this present moment, it may not be all too clear of where God is within our lives. But with some reflection we can see where he has been and where he has walked within us on our life's journey.

Tomorrow is an uncertain day and often the fruit of amendment is very small, giving us to frightful thoughts of death and the hereafter. Perhaps it will be more dangerous to live longer after we have amended so little in our thoughts and vices? But then again, a long life doesn't always make us perform better and only adds to our own guilt.

But life has a simple rule. For all of us, in all situations, it's putting one foot in front of the other and learning how to walk, trusting in God where we will care to place our foot in each step we take. Beware of curious and unprofitable searchings into this most profound sacrament, taking care not to sink into the depths of doubt.

Believe God is always able to do more than any of us can understand and humble your inquiry after truth, which is always ready to be taught. Don't become anxious or hold dispute with your thoughts, nor answer your doubts which only the devil suggests. But believe the words of the prophets and the people who put their faith in God. And the wicked enemy shall flee from you.

The bleakness and hardness of man's own heart, which tends only to think on what is of the present, fails to grasp the things to come, questioning what benefit is it to live longer when we amend so little of our vices.

A long life doesn't always make us better, only adding to our guilt and shame, if we only would have behaved ourselves well, even for one day. For while we are able to do many good things while we are well, when we become old and sick we know not what we will be able to do. This time in our life is very precious, although it is to be greatly lamented that we do not spend more of our time profitably. I greatly fear the time will come when we would wish for one part of the day or minute to amend justly and I don't know whether we will obtain it.

It is important, then, not to trust in our friends or family for the welfare of our souls; knowing that it is better now to provide a time and send some sort of good before us than to trust in others ever in helping after our death.

Death is the end of all; and our life passes suddenly away like that of a shadow. And only we truly deceive ourselves through our inordinate love of our flesh; after all, what else but our very own sin will the fire devour?

There is no vice which will not have its proper torment within the conscience of man. Wherein the proud will only be filled with utter confusion and torment, and us with the most miserable of want.

Nothing can be more exalted than the simplicity of obedience, where a pure and good conscience is a greater subject of overwhelming peace and joy than any learned philosophy. Learn to suffer little things, so that we may be delivered from more grievous suffering.

Remember then: a fervent and diligent man is ready for all things, working towards resisting the passions and vices of our flesh.

Watch over yourself and, whatever becomes of others, don't neglect yourself.

6

Conversing Within

The kingdom of God is within you. All too often we search the scriptures of religion, hoping to find God within, a hidden character within the many scripts and each rich in characters of its portrayal to the intrepid searcher.

If only we would turn our hearts to God, who dwells among us from within and rid this miserable world of all its outward solutions, we would surely find rest.

Learn to despise outward things and give yourself to things inward, and you'll begin to experience and see the Kingdom of God from within. Christ will come to you, showing you his own consolation, if you only ask and begin to prepare a fit and worthy place to dwell within you.

God makes many visits to the internal man and so sweet is his communing with us, delightful his consolation, plentiful his peace, and his familiarity becomes exceeding wonderful. It is therefore imperative that we possess some of the right spirit within us on our inner search towards finding a more spiritual life with our creator. Acknowledging that there is nothing that so defiles and entangles the heart of man as impure love of created things, having a good conscience will only enable God to sufficiently defend us in needed times.

For only he knows the time and the manner of delivering us from our vices, therefore we must resign ourselves to him and not become too disillusioned upon our waiting for deliverance. It belongs to God, to help and to deliver us all from any confusion and if we can but hold our own peace and suffer, we would see without doubt that the Lord will help us.

Often, it is extremely profitable for keeping us in greater humility that others know and reprehend our faults. And when a man is humbled for his defects, he appeases others and quickly satisfies those who are angry and bitter with him. Remember then, that God is a great protector of the humble and will deliver them; the humble he loves and comforts; and to the humble he inclines his precious grace, and after they have been cast down, will raise them to glory.

To the humble he reveals his secrets, inviting them towards himself. And to the humble, having been put to often great confusion, is well enough in peace, because they stand with the belief in God and not in the world.

Never think that you have made any progress, until you can look upon yourself as being inferior to all. We must keep ourselves first in peace and then we will be able to bring others towards peace. For a peaceable man can do more good than any of greater learning.

It is when we are without peace from within that we are discontented and disturbed, being tossed about with various suspicions; we are none too easy on ourselves and suffer no one else to be easy.

We all too often say what we were not intended to say and leave undone what it would be better for us to do. We'll consider what others are obliged to do and neglect that which we are ourselves are obliged to do.

We know all too well how to excuse and colour our own doings and we tend not to accept the excuses of others. It is therefore more just that we should accuse ourselves firstly and to excuse our brother and sister.

How far from charity and humility are we really, which knows no anger with anyone, or to have any indignation against anyone but oneself? It is no great thing to be able to live with the good and the meek of this world, for this is in itself naturally pleasing to all and everyone would willingly have that peace and only love those best who share and agree with our self. But to be able to share our love and affection and to be able to live peaceably with those who are tormented, and those who are harsh and perverse or disorderly, or even those who oppose us, is truly of a greater grace and should be worthy of high commendation.

There are those of us who keep themselves in peace and have peace with others. And there are some of us who are neither at peace within ourselves, nor suffer peace to be with others; they are troublesome towards others, but always of more trouble towards themselves. Then there are those who keep themselves in great peace and study to restore peace to others.

Yet all our peace in this miserable life is rather to be placed in humble suffering, than in not feeling adversities. You who know how to suffer will enjoy much peace. And such a one is a conqueror of himself, and lord of the world, a friend of Christ and an heir of heaven.

Simplicity and purity: with these things we are lifted to higher ground. Simplicity aims at God and must be the intention. Whereas, purity is in the affection that takes hold of him.

171

If only we were right in our own hearts, then every creature would become a looking-glass of life as well as a holy book of doctrine. And if we were full of goodness and pure from within, then we would discern all things without impediment and begin to understand them in the right manner.

The only thing that can penetrate heaven and hell is a pure heart. For when we begin to grow lukewarm, are we not afraid of a little labour and willingly take comfort in external things.

Only when we begin perfectly to overcome ourselves and to walk manfully in the way of God, do we make less account of those things which before us felt burdensome.

7

Consideration

I cannot trust much, if anything, to myself; because I often want grace and understanding and from within there is at times so little light and this is only to be quickly lost through negligence.

And so many times I can't ever perceive that I am so blind from within. I often do ill, but worse in excusing it. I am moved with great passions and mistake them for zeal; blame little things in others and begin to pass over greater things in myself.

I am all too quick at perceiving and weighing up of what I suffer from others, but tend not to mind in what others suffer in me. If only I could weigh my deeds duly, then perhaps I would have no room to judge others so harshly.

I sometimes struggle to become internal but realise also that unless I become devout in my search and begin to pass over in silence other men's concerns, looking particularly at myself, then I will be even further from the truth.

Where am I, when I am not present to myself? And when

I've deliberated and run over all things, what profit will it be to God if I've somehow neglected myself? I must therefore desire to have peace and true union with God and set all else aside, turning my eyes upon myself alone and setting myself free from all temporal care. Nothing must become great in my eyes, nothing high, nothing pleasant or agreeable, except it be purely God or of God.

God, who is eternal as well as incomprehensible, who fills all things, can afford true comfort to the soul and true joy to the heart. What I am, I am. And nothing can be greater than God sees me to be. I consider well of what is within myself and care not of what others say of me.

Only man considers the actions and beholds the face; but surely God looks upon the heart and weighs the intentions. I seek no open or outward testimony for myself only to show that plainly I have committed myself wholly to God. 'For not he that commendeth himself is approved, but whom God commendeth' (2 Cor. x, 18).

If I seek myself, I will only find myself and only unto my own ruin, for if I do not first seek God within myself, then I do more harm unto myself than would do the whole world and all its enemies.

It is a great art to know how to converse with Jesus; and to know how to keep him is even a greater wisdom. Be peaceable and humble, and God will be with you; devout and quiet and God will stay with you. It is not hard to despise all human comfort, when we have divine. But it is much, very much, harder to be able to want all comfort, both human and divine; and to be willing to bear this interior banishment for God's honour and to seek one's self in nothing, nor to think on one's own merit.

What great thing is it, if we become cheerful and devout,

when grace comes? Surely this hour would be desirable to all. For those who are carried by the grace of God, then let them ride with ease.

And of what wonder if he feels no weight, who is carried by the Almighty and led by the sovereign guide. A man must go through a long and great conflict within himself, before he can learn to overcome the vices and passions in himself fully, to begin to draw his whole affection towards God and when we stand upon our own, we easily decline after all passions and comforts of this world. But a true follower of God, a true searcher of Christ and a diligent pursuer of virtue, does not hunt after comforts, nor seek such sensible sweetnesses.

Therefore, when God gives his spiritual comfort, receive it with thanksgiving but know that it is the bounty of God, and not our merit. Don't be overjoyed or vainly presume, but rather be the more humble for this gift, and even the more cautious and fearful in all your actions; for this hour will shortly pass away and temptation surely follows. This is no new thing, nor is it strange to those who have experienced the ways of God. For when we feel God and his grace upon us we can say: 'In my abundance I said I shall never be moved', but when we feel that the grace of God has left us or has in some way been removed, we immediately say to ourselves: 'You O Lord have turned away your face from me, and now I have become troubled.'

Everyone has experienced this kind of vicissitude at one time or another. When comfort be taken away from you, don't despair but wait with humility and patience for the heavenly spirit to return; for God is able to restore a greater consolation.

If it has been like this for many, then we that are weak and poor must not become discouraged if we are sometimes fervent, or sometimes cold; because the spirit comes and goes according to its own good pleasure. For whether I have with me good men, or holy scriptures, faithful friends or even sweet singing and music; all these help little and give me but little relish when I feel forsaken by God's grace and left to dwell in my own pity and my own poverty.

At such a time there is no better remedy than patience, and denying oneself to the will of God. There is no one so religious and devout as not to have sometimes a withdrawal of grace, or even to feel a diminution of spirit within; certainly not highly wrapped or illuminated in anyway, as not to be tempted at first or at last.

For he is not worthy of the high contemplation of God who has not, for God's sake, been exercised with some tribulation. For temptation going before is usually a sign of ensuing consolation and heavenly comfort is promised to such as have been proved by temptation. We must therefore always prepare ourselves for a battle, for on our right hand and upon our left, are enemies that never rest.

8

Freedom Within

Spiritual consolations exceed all the delights of the world and pleasures of the flesh. For all my worldly delights are either vain or are obscured by the filth of a polluted mind. Spiritual delights are pleasant and honest, coming from virtue and infused by God to purify our minds. But these divine consolations are not to be enjoyed at will because temptations are never far from us.

Opposing these spiritual visits are a false freedom of mind and possessing a greater confidence in oneself.

God does well in giving us the grace and forgiveness in his consolation but we do ill in not ever returning it all to God, with thanksgiving. And for this reason, the many gifts given to us cannot begin to flow because we are so ungrateful towards the giver.

I would not have any such consolation as would rob me of all my compunction: nor do I wish to have such contemplation as to lead to pride.

For all that is high is not holy. Nor all that is pleasant

good. Nor every desire pure; neither is everything that is dear to us pleasing to God.

A discerning spirit, he that has been taught by the gift of grace and instructed by the scourge of its withdrawal, will not dare to attribute anything good to himself, but will rather acknowledge himself to be naked and poor.

Give to God what is his, and take to yourselves what is yours; that is, to give thanks to God for his grace; but as to ourselves, to be sensible that there is nothing to be attributed to us other than our own sin, and our punishment due to sin.

If we are to consider God and his dignity, no gift will seem little or unworthy; for it is not a small gift which is given by God. And though he does give punishment, it ought to be acceptable; for whatever he suffers to befall us, he will always do it for our salvation. And those who desire to retain the grace of God, let them be thankful for grace when it is given and patient when it is withdrawn. Pray that it may return; but be cautious and humble, lest you lose it.

God has many companions at his table and lovers of his heavenly kingdom; but really few bearers of the cross. Many are desirers of comfort, very few are willing to suffer with him. Many indeed seem to reverence his miracles, and more appear to love him as long as they meet with no adversity along the way; and of course there are those of us who will bless one another as long as we ourselves receive some kind of good fortune along the way in return. But when God decides to hide himself from us for a little while we begin to feel excessive dejection and fill ourselves with endless complaints.

We must try to love for love's sake, and not for any comfort in return, to accept his love for us as we are and love God no less in tribulation or anguish of our own hearts than in the greatest consolation received.

And if he should never give them his comfort, yet
  would they
Always praise him and give him thanks.
                    Imitation of Christ, Thomas à Kempis

We very seldom find anyone so spiritual as to be stripped of all things, for who shall be able to find the man that is truly poor in spirit and divested of all affection to creatures?

And of myself? If I were to give my whole substance, it would be nothing, and to do great penance would be little. Or if I would attain to myself all knowledge, I would still be far off. To have great wisdom and virtue and to be able to exceed in being devoted, then there would be still so much wanting in me.

> Go where you will and seek what you desire.
> But you will never ever find a higher way
> Above, not even a safer way below
> Than the way of God.

There is much that we must dispose of from within our infested minds and body. And each must order them away according only to his own will and as he seems best. And if we find something to suffer, willingly or unwillingly, so shall we still find God and the way of the Cross.

For either we shall begin to feel pain within our body and of its afflictions, or sustain deep within our very soul great tribulations and trials of the spirit.

Sometimes we all feel that God has left us to wallow in our own devices and has in some way abandoned us, at other times we may feel afflicted or persecuted by our neighbours; but more often we shall become trouble to ourselves.

Neither can we it seems be delivered or eased by some remedy or comfort, but as long as it shall please God we must bear it. For God would have us to learn to suffer tribulation without comfort and wholly to submit ourselves to him, to become more humble by trials. No one has so lively a feeling of the passion of Christ as them who happen to suffer such like things.

The Cross therefore appears to be always ready, and everywhere waits for us. There is no escape from it wherever we choose to run; for wherever we go, we carry it with ourselves as a part of ourselves.

Confusion turns us from all sides and everywhere we shall find the Cross and from everywhere we must out of necessity express patience if we desire inward peace and would merit an eternal crown.

And if we would carry it willingly, it would in fact carry us and bring us to our desired end; that place where there will be an end to all suffering, though here there will be no end.

To carry it unwillingly, we only achieve an unnecessary burden to ourselves; nevertheless we must bear it. If we were to fling away one cross, we would undoubtedly find another, perhaps more heavy.

Dare we, therefore, think that we can escape that which no mortal can ever avoid? Who was and is ever in this world without his personal cross and affliction to bear? And how dare we pretend to seek another way than this which is the way towards God.

And yet this mortal earthly being, who in so many ways is afflicted, is not without some alloy of comfort for their ease, because he may become sensible of the great profit which he gains by being able to bear his affliction.

For while he so willingly resigns himself to it, much of the burden of affliction and trial is converted into an assured hope of comfort from God and the more this flesh is brought down by dreadful afflictions, then the more the spirit is strengthened by an inner grace from God.

And it is with this that often it will gain such strength through its own desire of tribulation and through adversity, from the pure love of conformity towards God, as not to be willing to be without some kind of suffering; because it believes itself to be so much the more acceptable to God, as it shall be able to bear even greater things for him.

This is not man's virtue, but God's grace, which can and does affect great things in all frailty of flesh. Nor is it in accordance with human nature to bear afflictions, nor to chastise the body and begin to bring it under any subjection; to suffer reproaches, or to suffer any adversities or losses and to desire no prosperity in this world; and if we carefully look into ourselves we cannot of ourselves, do anything with it.

But if we begin to confide in God, strength will be given us and the world and the flesh shall be made subject to us.

We must prepare ourselves to suffer many diverse evils of this miserable life along with adversities; so it is with us, wherever we are and whoever we are, indeed will we all find it, wherever we chose to hide ourselves.

The Hungers of the Soul

Whispers of the world! Calling and beaconing the soul
   to deceive.
Why can't I forget sweet dreams of you?
Every night I go through unpleasant dreams
Why can't I forget you and start my life anew?
Instead of having unpleasant dreams of you.

You never loved me, it's plain.
I should know, I'll never ever be the same.
I should hate you, the whole day through, instead
Of having these sweet dreams of you.

Things that I know, things I did cannot ever become
   true
Why can't I forget the past and start my life anew?
Instead of having unpleasant dreams of you.

Happy ears, happy ears indeed, which receive the accents of

the divine whisper speaking within, and take no notice of the whisperings of the past. And hear the truth itself teaching within and not the voice that sounds without.

Is our hunger for holy doctrine a mystery? Is there some peculiar secret that lies behind it? Whenever we talk of our sanctification we undoubtedly always look for a greater mystery; some sort of mystery apart from that which must ever be so mysterious wherever the Holy Spirit works, some spiritual occult experience which only the initiated know.

There are thousands upon thousands of people who go to church every Sunday hoping to solve for themselves this great mystery. At conferences or at meetings, many times they have reached the very brink of what they have thought to be the enlightened answers to many of their questionable thoughts, but then somehow no further revelations came. Poring over religious books and dogmas, how often are we not within a paragraph or two of finding it? Perhaps the next page or the next sentence will reveal all, and we would be borne on that flowing tide for ever. But nothing happened. The next sentence along with the next pages were read but still it eludes us; though the promise of its coming was kept faithfully until the end, the last chapter finds us still pursuing.

Why did nothing happen? Because there was nothing to happen. Or at least nothing of the kind of thing we were looking for. And why does it elude us? Perhaps because there was no 'it'. When shall we learn that the hunger of our souls and the pursuit of holiness is simply the pursuit of God? When shall we substitute for the 'it' of a fictitious aspiration the approach of a living friend? Our sanctity is in character and not in moods; divinity is in our own plain and calm humanity, and in no mystic rapture of the soul.

And yet there are those who, for exactly a contrary reason, will find scant satisfaction here.

Their complaint is not that a religion or a certain doctrine expressed in terms of friendship is too homely, but that it is still too mystical. To 'abide' in Christ, to 'make Christ our most constant companion' is to them the purest mysticism. They want something absolutely tangible and absolutely direct. These are not the poetical souls who seek a sign, a mysticism in excess; but the prosaic natures whose want is probably mathematical definitions and details.

Friendship of one another is the nearest thing we know to what religion is to man. God is love. And to make religion and doctrine akin to friendship is to simply give it the highest expression conceivable by man. The beauty of friendship is its infinity, and one can never evacuate life of mysticism. Our homes should be full of it, and love is full of it, religion is certainly full of it.

Why should we begin to stumble at what in the relation of man to God is natural in the relationship of man toward his fellow man? Some of us cannot ever begin to conceive or realise a mystical relationship with God, and perhaps all that can be done for them is to come across it by stepping on to it by a still plainer analogy from common life.

All thorough work is slow, as is all true development of character. We should not think that nothing is happening because we fail at times to see ourselves grow, or even hear the whirr of the machinery from within. The inward man is renewed from day to day and undoubtedly the higher the structure, the slower the progress in perfecting the soul.

To await the growing of our soul, nevertheless, is an almost divine act of our faith. How pardonable, surely, the impatience of deformity within itself, of a consciously despicable character standing before Christ, wondering, yearning, hungering to be like that? Yet we must learn to trust the process fearlessly and without any misgiving.

The tempting expedient is, in haste for abrupt or visible progress, to try some method less spiritual, or to defeat the end by watching for effects instead of keeping the eye on the cause. The creation of a new heart, as with the renewing of a right spirit, is an omnipotent work of God. And 'He which hath begun a good work in you will perfect it unto that day'. A religion or doctrine of any effortless adoration may be a religion for an angel but never for mankind. Not in the contemplative, but only in the active lies true life; and not in the realm of ideals but among tangible things is mankind's sanctification wrought.

Resolution, self-crucifixion, agony, pain and effort – all the things already dismissed as being futile in themselves must now be restored to office, and an element of responsibility laid upon them. And what of their office? Nothing less than to move the vastness of inertia of the soul and place it and keep it where the spiritual forces will act upon it. It is to rally the forces of our will and keep the surface of the mirror bright and always in position. It is to uncover the face which is to look at Christ, and to draw down the veil when unhallowed sights are near.

This is a methodical world in which we live, and not in my opinion an accidental world: nothing that happens in the world happens by sheer chance. I believe that everything is arranged upon definite principles, and nothing should be attributed to mere random choice.

Everything is governed by law. Even the religious world and all its teachings and doctrines from many denominations is governed by its own laws. Our character and of others is governed by law, along with our own happiness.

Do you expect faith/happiness/peace/rest to literally drop down from a hidden height like rain? We, as only human, tend to forget this, expecting them to drop into our souls and, even if they did, they would no less have their origin in previous activities and be controlled by some natural laws, or would be mature effects of former causes.

Equally everything has a previous history and our own character is subjected to this in its expectations. Storms and winds and calms from within are not in my opinion accidents, but brought about by antecedent circumstances. Rest and peace are but calms in man's inward nature, and arise through causes as definite and as inevitable.

So it is with the making of Christian experiences. Certain laws are followed; certain effects are the result. These effects cannot but be the result, but the result can never take place without the previous cause. To expect results without antecedents is to expect bread without ingredients. That impossibility is precisely an almost universal expectation.

As I look back upon the past years of my life, it is true that my unhappiness has chiefly come about from a succession of personal mortifications and trivial disappointments. Great trials came at lengthened intervals, and I would rise to engage them; but it is the petty friction of my everyday life, the jar of work or business, the discord of the domestic circle, the collapse of my ambitions, the crossing of my resolutions and the taking down of my own conceit, which makes inward peace impossible at times.

And now my wounded vanity, then disappointed hopes, unsatisfied selfishness – these are the old vulgar, universal sources of man's unrest.

Christianity is a fine inoculation, a transfusion of healthy blood into an anaemic or poisoned soul. To me, Christianity is

186

almost an art – to teach us the art of life. Its whole curriculum lies in a few words – 'Learn of Me' and, unlike most education, this becomes almost purely personal; it is not to be had from books or lectures or creeds or doctrines. It is a study from life. Christ never said much in mere words about the Christian graces. He lived them, because he *was* them.

Glossary

OC	Officer Commanding
CO	Commanding Officer
RTU	Return to unit
TAB	Tactical advance into battle (forced route march)
OP	Observation post
Bivvy	Bivouac/camp without tents
Marche ou crève	March or die
Rangers	French army boots
Cherry beret	Red beret worn by the Parachute Regt
SAS	Special Air Squadron (Guards Squadron, 22nd Regt)
G Squadron	Guards Squadron (22ns Ind. Para. Regt) 'Pathfinder'
PJI	Parachute jump instructor